God Is For You

By

Thad Riley

Table Of Contents

Foreword by J.R. Gwartney

I met Thad Riley on a hot summer day in 2005 in Jackson TN. My son, Gage, was on the same tee-ball team as his daughter, Kaitlin, and as anyone who has seen a 5-year-olds tee-ball game can attest to, we spent our time laughing as a dozen kids ran around the infield aimlessly chasing a baseball. I noticed one huge guy with an equally huge personality yelling at his daughter to run the other way round the bases. I commented that if the oversized helmet were the right size, then maybe it wouldn't fall over her eyes and she'd actually know which direction she was trying to run. He bellowed out a laugh and that's all it took. We became fast friends and by the third game we were meeting up for pizza after the games and learning about each other's families.

The Rileys had recently moved to Jackson and I was immediately struck by how many different jobs this guy had already accumulated. He'd been in sales, management, retail, tech and who knew what else, but he certainly didn't seem like a flaky, wishy-washy person. The Riley's were only in Jackson for a couple of years and if my math is right, I watched him go through 3 different jobs while he was here. He wasn't fired or let go from any of these positions and every move was a promotion, but Thad was always on the lookout for the next big thing. It didn't take me long to notice 2 things about Thad – He loves new challenges, and he never stops searching. Now these 2 qualities can be a problem for some people. You might think I'm describing a guy who drops his responsibilities to run after every shiny new challenge, but there's one more quality that I noticed in Thad that kept him grounded - Thad always sees God work in the everyday, ordinary events.

Many of us (like myself) are afraid of change - We get comfortable with our routine. Now there's nothing wrong with routine. It oftentimes keeps us on task and dependable. But sometimes routine keeps us from responding to God's calling. Routine often robs us of the adventure that awaits the person who is willing to answer the call. Thad was never a fan of routine. The result is a life full of ups and downs, laughter and heartache, joy and pain, all the while finding God at work in every peak and valley.

What is this book all about? It's not only about courageously answering God's call on your life, it's about finding God at work all around us. Ferris Bueller from the movie *Ferris Bueller's Day Off* was right when he said, "Life moves pretty fast. If you don't stop and look around once in a while, you could miss it." Sure, we look for God in major trials or tragedy, but do we seek His providence in traffic, grocery shopping, or at the dentist office? The following pages are not only about the trials and triumphs that have shaped my friend's life, but also about finding God at work at a tee-ball game.

Prelude

Dear Larry,

There's a good chance I'm the last person you ever expected to hear from, and I'm hoping somehow God gets this to you. Your letter came to me almost twenty years ago and I've read it a hundred times, probably even a few more. I didn't want to write you back at the time, maybe because I was too young and proud to take in what you were trying to tell me. The years, however, have shown me the wisdom, love, and grace you forged into my life, and that one letter still means everything to me.

Did you know I saved it for years and years? It's just so true! It was placed neatly under the film strips in my photo album, that one photo album that contains the highlights of my life. Did you have one of those? Knowing you, your album would have been packed with more pictures of the people you cared about than yourself. Mine is a crazy mish mash of some of the stories from my life, though most of it is pretty lighthearted fun. What my old photo album doesn't display, this book most certainly does because I guess those stories deserved to have their own home, too.

My friend, there is some pretty raw brokenness within these pages, but the greatest of triumphs is often only a turn of the page away. My most sincere hope is to bring the story of Jesus into our world today, and share with everyone how much God has done for me. Roughly half of this book takes us on the journey into the last days of the life of Jesus because you, more than anyone, knew that people need to know who Jesus is and how much he is still working all around us. Even in ... no, *especially* in our brokenness, he is working, just like he did two thousand years ago within the brokenness of his world. But these pages are definitely not all gloom and doom, my friend, because life isn't just one melancholy moment after another. I hope you'll laugh a little, and there are some pages where you might even want to jump up and let out a hearty cheer. There's a sweet undercurrent of optimism here, which I know would be right up your alley.

I know writing you back is a strange way to start my book, but I missed my chance here on earth, which is something I'll always regret. My other big regret is losing your letter, which must have happened at some point in the past few years. One day I went to pull it out again for another read, but the space it was in was tragically empty and I haven't been able to find it anywhere. It was only a little over two years after you sent me the letter that your life was taken in that devastating accident. We were so disconnected in those last days that I didn't find out for weeks after your funeral what had happened. I missed my chance to tell you goodbye, but you and I know it was never going to be goodbye anyway.

Larry, would you ask God to come alongside anyone who picks up this book and tell him I'm hoping this will be a great encouragement to them? He knows my heart, even before I know my own heart, and he completely knows why I wrote all of this, but maybe you all could talk about this, too. Thank you, my friend.

I miss you,

Thad

Chapter 1

A New Adventure

"Make your choice, adventurous Stranger,

Strike the bell and bide the danger,

Or wonder, till it drives you mad,

What would have followed if you had."

\- C.S. Lewis, *The Magician's Nephew*

It was 4:30 a.m. on May 30th, 1992. A few stuffed-full plastic crates, a tattered suitcase, and my new gym bag were crammed into the interior of my mint green, 1986 Subaru GL Sport. I could barely keep down the wild feelings of anticipation surging through me. I felt like a kid about to go down the biggest water slide you'd ever seen, ready to scream "Woo-Hoo!" from the top of my lungs. My hands and feet moved in a flurry as I frenetically shoved the last few items recklessly into my trunk. This was it! The moment had finally arrived to embark on the summer adventure of a lifetime. I was heading to Virginia Beach for a missions project with the college organization Campus Crusade for Christ, today known as CRU. Never before had I spent any serious time away from my home, and now, as a twenty year old ready to take on the world, the timing could not have been better.

My mother stood to dad's left, quietly watching me double and triple check that everything had found its place somehow into my car. With her forehead tense and lips clenched, she seemed more concerned for my safety than anything, but she didn't need to be. My parents never gave their approval for my adventure that summer, but that didn't slow me down. They saw me as an impulsive young man, making life altering decisions at the drop of a hat! In my favor, though, I possessed confidence, optimism, and enthusiasm for life, and that should have counted for something. Well, at least to me it did. If I was to be thrown headfirst into this world, I had decided the best place for a college guy to do this was on Summer Project in Virginia Beach.

Dad stood by the door between the house and the garage with his blue eyes just staring at me, slowly shaking his head back and forth. "Your mother and I always feared you'd try to do something like this," was all he could quietly muster in my last moments with them. My parents, especially my father, were opposed to the idea of me spending the entire summer away. Dad thought this was a complete waste of time, and he wasted no time of his own in sharing this with me a few months earlier when I told him my intentions.

"People like us don't do these missions or trips," Dad told me the moment I enthusiastically greeted him with the news of my summer plans.

"People like us have real jobs and make real money," he said.

In the world where I was raised, this decision was risky and didn't make any sense. In the world I was passionately pursuing, this was the only way to live. I never believed the world needed another young gun to shoot his way out of college with a shiny new business degree, launching himself into my father's "real world", making stacks of money. It was time for me to close my eyes, take a deep breath, and jump. Everyone kept worrying about where I would land. I just wanted to fly.

Even though Dad railed against this adventure, my passion to pursue it wasn't going to be easily snuffed out. My father was an intelligent and successful man who could sell anything to anybody, except maybe to his own son. I was never a big believer in living a life like Dad, one of financial success, where you were respected for your results and not the man you were. Life seems too short and too important to make this all about money. As a twenty year old guy who travelled to serve kids in the poorest parts of America, rode skateboards until they broke, and jumped off any big rock I could find on the shores of the Cumberland River, I knew my existence had to be so much more than a satisfying career and a big check. Wasn't it possible God had different plans for me than just getting a job that paid a bunch of money? If he didn't, then what was the point of this life? There had to be more.

Dad's words rolled off of me as I reversed down the driveway and shifted my car into drive. It wasn't the first time Dad and I didn't agree about my life, so this wasn't my first ride at this rodeo. Dad was passionate about other things, and those things never held much appeal to me. The feeling, I'm sure, was quite mutual. He was a high school athlete, lettering in baseball and football, but music and the arts and playing basketball with my friends floated my boat. Dad was brilliant and one of the best financial planners in the country, but I didn't want to follow in his footsteps. There was a much different road I needed to walk, though I had no clue what it might be. I was going down this path with or without his support, because this was exactly what gung-ho, freewheeling college guys do.

Back in those primitive days of the early 1990's, before Google Maps and navigation, journeys like this were a little more exciting. I had never been to the state of Virginia before, and the lush mountains and green forests were a welcome sight for my sore eyes. To say I was through the roof might have been an understatement. As I journeyed from the Midwest to the East Coast, and even though I drove one hundred and eleven miles in the wrong direction (Hello Baltimore! ...and goodbye Baltimore!), nothing could deflate my spirits. For the record, I just used Google Maps to show me exactly how far out of the way I drove on that day twenty-five years ago. Maybe we've taken all the adventure out of road trips, but we have surely saved broke college guys a few bucks in gas money!

With the windows down and the wind whipping through my hair, I cruised down the highway, belting out songs from my CD player like Arrested Development's "Tennessee", Styx's "Blue Collar Man", and Garth Brooks' "The Dance". What should have been a fairly easy, less than ten hour drive turned into twelve hours of intense and life-changing karaoke. Dreams of making new friends and the memories of a lifetime raced through my mind, and a new adventure by the ocean was certainly calling my name. I didn't know a soul in Virginia Beach, and I was quite thrilled with the idea of a fresh start and new friendships. This would be the greatest summer of my life, and I was ready for everything it had to offer.

Of the sixty participating students, I was one of the last to arrive at the project houses, and my new friends greeted me with huge smiles, high fives, and warm hugs. There was Peter from Maine, Matt from California, and Sean from Virginia. I met Betsy from Ohio, Georgia from Colorado, and Jane from Alabama. My smile stretched ear-to-ear as I was introduced to new housemates from all walks of life from all across the country. From Chico State to the University of New Hampshire they came, thirty guys and thirty girls living in two houses just a few blocks from the Atlantic Ocean. I had never been in a situation with this much potential for so many new friendships, and I wasn't going to be the last person to jump on board!

Growing up as the hyper kid trying to get attention by being funny or a bit out of control wasn't the best recipe for winning popularity contests. Good friendships weren't a common thing in my early years, and those past rejections still affected me in college. More often than not, being an overweight kid left me as the last kid picked on a team at recess and as one of the top targets in my school for the bullies. For the record, my mother refused to call me chubby or fat, only referring to me as being big boned. Occasionally she'd say I was husky, which wasn't the worst thing, but sharing a term of identity with a dog or the larger size of boy's pants at Kmart didn't exactly build my self esteem or bring in new friends by the truckload. I guess you could say throughout my childhood there always seemed to be plenty of seats around me at the lunch table. With a thankful heart, I can say life changed suddenly my sophomore year of high school, but that story is for another time and another chapter. From the greeting I received upon my arrival at project, I could tell my new fellow residents of Virginia Beach were as thrilled as I was to be there.

Before we could blink, the transition was over and we were all settled in. After only a few days, we were being challenged in new roles and duties and were getting into a pretty good flow. Our community of sixty students got in sync, and we connected as friends and as young followers of Jesus who were brought together for a purpose. Some mornings you could see twenty of us down on the beach on our knees as the God who created the sunrise over the Atlantic listened lovingly to our chorus of prayers. Sometimes we asked Him for help, sometimes we thanked Him for the day, and sometimes we were overwhelmed with gratefulness for his deep love for us. Many nights I was on the beach long after the sun set, listening to the waves and a story from one of my new friends. Maybe too often those stories were somewhat familiar, yet still so different from my own. I discovered we all had so much in common, yet each one of us was very unique.

"I have an IQ of over 160," he told us flatly.

One of the project staff, a lady named Lola, was my partner for the evening, and we headed to the boardwalk as soon as dinner was over. As a pair of friends, it was easy for us to approach individuals and small groups as they strolled by us on those warm, summer nights. Our purpose was to share the story of Jesus and tell anyone who'd listen of how much God loves them. We had approached several different people, but no one seemed much for conversation on this perfect June evening. That's when we saw him, just as the sun crept away behind us and the moon rose over the ocean. The little man walked alone, and seemed to be wandering a bit, as if heading nowhere.

After a quick prayer under my breath, Lola nodded to me, and we approached him. He seemed tiny, as opposed to my looming six foot stature, and if he was an inch over five and a half feet tall, I'd have been shocked. What hair little remained clung to the sides of his head, and his mustache looked a little like something out of the old show *Starsky and Hutch* (if you're too young for this, get on YouTube asap). He looked to be in his early forties, but my gut said he looked at least a few years older than he might have been.

"Hi there. How are you this evening?" I asked the man.

Crinkling his forehead, and tilting his head slightly at us, he responded, "I'm well. What can I do for you."

"My name is Thad, and this is my friend Lola," I said gesturing to my right. "Do you have a few minutes?"

Approaching someone you've never met before and striking up a conversation can be a bit intimidating. Doing it with the purpose of sharing your testimony of God's love and the story of Jesus can be even more so! After our brief introductions, Lola and I shared a little bit of our story with the man, and the more we opened up about our purposes of being here, the more intrigued he became.

Right off the bat he told us he was the founder of a technology company in Canada, and had taken a week for summer vacation on the shores of Virginia Beach. The pace of his speech increased, and suddenly he flew threw the details of his work, and quickly Lola and I were lost amidst his seemingly endless technical details. He might as well have been talking about fixing a car's engine or the mating habits of Greater Sage Grouse (again, you have Google available to you today, thus...). He saw our looks of confusion during his technical ramblings, and I'll never forget what he said next.

"I have an IQ over 160. And I know where this is going. I've studied the life of Jesus, and am not interested in religion."

"Me neither," replied Lola. 'I'm not interested in religion, but what about God. Do you believe in him? In your heart?"

The man stared back at us, looking about as shocked as a female Greater Sage Grouse (you did Google this, right?). I don't think he knew what to say. He had spent his whole life being the smartest guy in the room, but this wasn't a conversation about how much he knew, but what this brilliant man truly believed. He simply didn't know what to say, and all we were asking him about was his heart.

When I think of heart, I think about Rocky Balboa getting up off the mat after getting knocked down again by the giant Russian. Or the iconic movie moment when the utterly exhausted Samwise Gamgee lifted up Frodo Baggins and carried him to the top of Mount Doom so he could throw the Ring of Power into the fire. When I think of heart, I think of the greatest athletic moments in history, like Kerri Strug with that insane one-legged-landing on the vault in the 1996 Olympics or Jason Lezak overcoming a huge lead by the French and blowing away the fastest time in swimming's history to take home the gold in the men's 4X100 in the 2008 games. Sometimes it's not on a screen, but this heart thing happens in real life. Just a few weeks ago I was in line at the grocery store when a police officer in front of me saw an older gentleman short of money for his groceries. Before any of us could figure out what had happened, the officer left our line to pay whatever remained on the man's grocery bill and humbly returned to the groceries he'd left on the belt.

Heart. It was why I was so completely pumped to drive twelve hours (I know it should have been ten, but I never claimed to have any sense of direction, right?) and work hard to pay my own way so that I could love and serve people in Virginia Beach, Virginia. It's what motivates marathon runners to keep pushing a little farther and a little faster, even when their body is telling them it's impossible to take another step, but they still take one more step. It's what drives our purposes, and you can't add it up or turn it into an exact science. It's just simply heart.

This was our mission for the summer, our purpose, or whatever you want to call it. We were here for this, this moment when we could share the good news of Jesus with someone who really didn't understand or believe in their heart. It didn't matter who we came across or what their life was, we were there to be a conduit between them and God, in whatever way that might look. Basically, our mission was to be available to share the good news of Jesus from our heart to theirs. Nothing mattered more to us than this.

One of the most memorable stories I was scripted in was when we gave a little help to a lady who was on the run, living shelter to shelter for eleven years, to escape an abusive husband who knew no tenderness. In their last few years together, she only knew the right hook and cutting words from this man who was a leader in their town. She accepted the few dollars we could scrounge together, and a new white sweatshirt my Mom sent me that didn't quite fit, but that was about all she'd take. She told us she was still scared of him, and she was sure if she settled down anywhere he'd be able to find her.

I still think of her to this day, and pray for her when I can remember to. I really don't have a clue how her life has turned out, but maybe I wasn't supposed to know. The summer of 1992 was about being a part of what God was doing, and a big part of that meant letting go of the results. I was put there to share God's love, and that was most of the story, although later we will come to understand there was far more going on that summer than I could have even begun to imagine.

In pursuit of following this mission, we combed the beach looking for people like the brilliant man and the homeless woman. God's love and the hope He gives us was far too colossal for us to keep secret. We wanted to change the world, and we were trying to do it one person at a time. This wasn't an original idea. Actually, we were just following the lead of twelve men who did something similar. Two thousand years ago, the disciples of Jesus showed us what to do, what could be gained, and what losses they were ready to endure for the sake of knowing him.

According to the US Bureau of Labor, the average American employee works in their current job for just over four and a half years. Promises of better pay, better working conditions, and better benefits are often the impetus for change. In the days of Jesus, however, most careers lasted a lifetime. If you were a fisherman, you stayed a fisherman, and there was a great chance your kids would be fishermen. Despite this and without hesitation, the disciples walked away from their established careers to follow Jesus. They didn't know where they were going, and they didn't know how they would survive. All they knew was that they were going with Jesus.

Boats were ditched at the shore. Fishermen left their livelihoods. A tax collector left everything to follow Jesus, the same Jesus of whom it is said in Luke 9:58, "Foxes have holes, and birds of the air have nests, but the Son of Man has nowhere to lay his head." Yet when he said, "Follow me," they left everything behind and followed him.

No fish were found in Simon Peter's nets after a long night drifting in the deep waters. Sleep deprived and demoralized after a night's work yielding no bounty, he and his brother, Andrew, were exhausted. They had come ashore and were washing their nets when Jesus noticed their boat. A large crowd walked with Jesus and, as Luke 5:1 says, they started "pressing in on him." Out of room at the edge of the lake, Jesus jumped into Peter's empty boat, took a seat and began to teach to everyone who was following him.

There was just no way! Peter was stunned. Could this be the promised Messiah, the Savior of all men? He grabbed his brother, Andrew, and suddenly Jesus was telling these fishermen to leave everything behind and follow him. They left their boat on the shore and were gone. James and John were on a boat with their father, mending nets, when Jesus called them to follow him. Down went the nets as the brothers left everything behind to follow Jesus. Next was Nathaniel who exclaimed after just a few sentences from Jesus, "Rabbi, you are the Son of God! You are the King of Israel!" (John 1:49). Their lives were changed forever; they left everything behind and went with Jesus. "Follow me" was the opening and closing line, with nothing in between, but it was all Matthew needed to hear from the lips of Jesus. Matthew, a tax collector, and probably the last guy who would have been on anyone's list to become a disciple of Jesus, got up from his collecting booth and left everything to follow him.

None of this really makes sense, does it? Matthew might have been the only one with any financial security, but he left everything behind to be with Jesus. These fishermen left their possessions and livelihoods and nobody really knew where they were going or what would happen next. I wonder if James and John's Dad had something to say to them when they walked away from him. I wonder if he was confused and just stood there shaking his head, just like my father two thousand years later. I hope he didn't. I hope he saw what they saw. I hope deep down he knew in his heart the same thing I knew two millenniums later. There truly is no stopping someone who has made the decision to follow Jesus.

Despite my parents disapproval and the risks I was taking, I never considered missing out on that Summer Project in 1992, and there is no reason to believe any of the disciples didn't run after Jesus with joy and enthusiasm. Their eagerness jumps off the page as we see these men go with him down what is about to become a very wild and dangerous path. Men and women like this aren't common and too often we can make following Jesus seem more confusing than it actually is. When we consider the cost of following Jesus, as I'm sure each of the disciples did, how do you decide where to draw the line? Maybe a better question is: who is really drawing this line for you? Is the world around you defining whether or not the cost is too great for you to truly follow Jesus?

Not long after the day when Jesus said, "Follow me", he told his disciples, "Go." For now, he had invited them to come with him and their adventure began when they truly left everything behind. Jesus was going to lead them on a journey where they would see miracles of water turned into wine, a few loaves and fish feeding five thousand people, a man being raised from the dead, and lepers healed. Jesus did this for the purpose of bringing glory to the Father, as he told us in John 12:27-

28. The disciples came and were now on the most intense and unpredictable ride they could have ever imagined. The calling on their lives was direct, but it was most certainly not exclusive.

The summer of '92 was an important time in my life to establish a deep love for God, to spend my time in community, and to take a chance and just go. It was one the greatest summer's of my life, and it is moments like these that I lean on during the hard times. When we decide to be like the disciples and just go, we grow in our faith and prepare ourselves for what battles and challenges might lay ahead.

There will be a day when Jesus will also tell you, "Go," or maybe he already has. Maybe, though, just maybe, right now he is telling you to come to him, to leave behind the life you have always known and to embrace him and his love. Maybe this just brings on more questions, and hopefully over the next several pages you can begin to encounter Jesus and discover the answers you're seeking. For over two thousand years no one else in the history of the world has had such a powerful and deeply personal impact on all of mankind. He is the promised Messiah and the Savior of the world.

Chapter 2

The Silence is Deafening

"The greatest disease in the West today is not TB or leprosy; it is being unwanted, unloved, and uncared for. We can cure physical diseases with medicine, but the only cure for loneliness, despair, and hopelessness is love. There are many in the world who are dying for a piece of bread but there are many more dying for a little love. The poverty in the West is a different kind of poverty -- it is not only a poverty of loneliness but also of spirituality. There's a hunger for love, as there is a hunger for God."

- Mother Teresa

Boredom didn't even begin to describe it. Working for years as a manager in the cell phone industry was a tough enough gig, but this quiet day in the summer of 2014 felt like it would never end. Our store was already too big for the amount of customers coming in, and today I felt like a kid standing on a pitcher's mound in an empty stadium as, "HELLO, Hello, hello," echoed gently through the empty bleachers and around the snack bars. We didn't have a snackbar in the cell phone store, of course, but there was a Circle K just out back, and they had large sodas for fifty-nine cents. It didn't make up for not having the glorious scent of ballpark hotdogs and those warm peanuts, but it was a far better price on soda than you'd get at the stadium. Summertime daydreaming about my Chicago Cubs and hotdogs came to an abrupt halt when Alice pulled open the door, heralding our full attention. Standing close to the front of the store, I greeted her immediately.

"Good afternoon!" I said with a smile. "What brings you into our neck of the woods today?"

"Well, this is my first smart phone. I know you probably think I'm stupid, but this thing makes no sense."

"Ma'am, I hear this all the time," I said with big grin. "We help people every day get a handle on their smartphones, so you're definitely not stupid, okay?"

The lady's complaints were a common theme in our industry, especially with some of our older customers. I always enjoyed hanging out and spending time with them, and I had a pretty good understanding of how to make them feel more comfortable with their phone or with their plan. My boss even joked about how I would sit on a bench with an older person for hours and hours. We'd talk about the phones, sure, but there were grandkids and friends in Florida and vacations on giant cruise ships to hear about. This was where I was at my best, so I was quite glad to help my new friend.

She smiled, breathing a sigh of relief and said, "Thank you. If you can just help me figure this thing out, that would be great. I'm Alice."

I smiled back and said, "I'm Thad. It's nice to meet you, Alice!"

I motioned for her to have a seat with me on a nearby bench. We sat down together and I started asking her a few questions so I could figure out how to best help her. As I gathered information from Alice, I realized she knew nothing about her phone.

"Alice, do you know how to make a phone call?" I asked. She paused for a moment and then answered me saying, "I don't need to. I don't have anyone to call and nobody calls me anymore."

She didn't seem uncomfortable at all when she said it, but I certainly was! I tried not to show it, but a sudden wave of sadness came over me. I didn't know anything about her story, but I was shocked that such a nice, older lady was telling me she had no one to talk to. I moved on quickly, though, and I walked through some smart phone basics and was surprised at how quick she was picking things up. She said she didn't usually ask for help, and she was glad she took a chance. We sat on the bench right next to each other for a while. I listened and we joked until we felt like old friends with nothing better to do than sit in a store. As our conversation drifted back to her phone, she began to share a little bit more as she opened up about her life.

"Well, the reason I don't need to learn about calling is because I never call anyone. I don't have anyone," the white-haired, older lady softly spoke, this time expressing her sadness. "My husband and son have both passed away, and the only one left in my family is my daughter, and we don't talk anymore. We used to talk a lot. Every morning she called me on her way to work, for years and years, but after a while she stopped calling as much, and eventually she just never called me again. I don't have anyone."

"I'm sorry, Alice. I'm truly sorry," I said quietly.

"It's ok," she said with a heavy sigh as her shoulders slumped a little forward. Looking back up at me, she said, "I guess I don't mind as much anymore."

We sat for several more minutes as she quietly shared a few stories. After she finished and was feeling much more comfortable with her phone, I gave her my card and told her to call me anytime. I don't think she will ever call me, though. I'll never forget her words and how her appearance changed when she spoke about the losses of those she once loved.

How had it come to this for Alice? Didn't she want something so much more in the last years of her life? She seemed so resigned to not having anyone close to her, and it just didn't make any sense to me. We were created and made for connections, and it's in those deeper connections that we truly experience the best this life has to offer. My friend Alice had thrown in the towel and given up, and I couldn't understand. Couldn't she just call her daughter, if only to say hi after all of these years of nothing? I was deeply sad for Alice and her story still deeply moves me to this very day.

Loneliness is a pretty big problem in our culture. Technology has disabled the human touch and, instead of a warm, personal connection to others, we are more apt to resort to the more cool methods of texting or messaging our friends. There is something about hearing someone's voice that connects us, yet it is becoming less and less of the norm in our society today.

Many struggle with loneliness, and I wonder if the story of Alice isn't as rare as we would like to believe. It truly breaks my heart to think a lady who might live only a few more years will possibly spend those days without any real connection to anyone else. How does someone exist like this? How can we so easily accept it when mothers and fathers and sons and daughters and brothers and sisters and the best of friends are no longer a part of our lives?

I never saw my friend, Alice, after that day, but I hope one day we can find a bench to sit down on again. She seemed a little happier as she walked out the door with one phone number she knew would always have a friendly voice on the other end of the line. It's been a few years, though, and I haven't heard from her. I am grateful for the brief moment of understanding we shared. I am hopeful she will embrace the idea of being close to people again, but I'm not sure she will. I wish she could have met my friend, Larry. He would have known what to say to Alice.

Larry Clark will be one of the first people I want to see when I go to heaven. I have missed my friend for almost twenty years now and would give almost anything to answer his final letter to me. I met Larry at Willowcreek Community Church in South Barrington, Illinois. A couple of my friends and I from the Axis Ministry, a now-defunct Gen X ministry we launched in 1995, had this idea of starting a pick-up basketball game with a Bible study time afterward, and before we knew it, we had about sixty dudes. The guys who came were anywhere from eighteen to thirty years old, and it was the rough, open gym style of basketball you might expect it to be. Afterwards, we would go back to one of the guy's houses, eat a bunch of topping-overloaded pizza, break into four or five small groups, and open up the Bible and dive in.

There were many lifelong friendships developed from those days, but nothing else was quite like my friendship with Larry. He wasn't the first one to join our group, but once he saw what we were all about, he was one hundred percent in. Larry decided to start coming to my small group study and quickly fit in with the rest of the guys. He didn't play basketball very often with us and really was much more interested in our time together in fellowship and in the study of God's word. Larry was the oldest one there, probably in his mid thirties, and had quite a story himself.

What peaked Larry's interest the most, however, was hearing other's stories. I guess that's just who my friend was. It was probably about two months after he joined the group I discovered he was living off a severance package from a job he had a while ago, and that he was a full time volunteer at Willowcreek. Larry was an incredible listener and an even better friend. He was always present and never hogged the spotlight. My friend liked to hang back and be there to encourage while also pushing us in new directions spiritually.

It was the Fall of 1996, and both the group and I were changing. After roughly a year of being a leader and encourager within the ministry, I was offered an internship within Axis. After some prayer and counsel, I knew it was time for me to move on and to step aside as another Small Group Leader would now take my place. I left my small group to help launch the new College Ministry, but that position didn't last long. Just a few months after I started, I screwed up and the fall was quite hard.

It was more than a mistake, more than some simple little problem. I knew what I had done was wrong, and as soon as it happened, I was overcome with guilt. Until that day, I was a virgin, prepared to one day enter a marriage on the best terms possible. I knew having sex with my girlfriend was a huge mistake, but I still made the wrong decision. Regret consumed me, and I went to my leaders and immediately confessed. In my mind, I didn't deserve to be on staff anymore and wanted to resign my position as an intern. After years of having a personal relationship with God and being raised in the church, I knew I had totally allowed sexual sin to get a hold of me. There was no doubt in my mind that this was not God's best for me. My leaders walked through repentance with me, but they did not at all want me to resign. They wanted me to stay in community and to just go through a process of repentance while they surrounded me in prayer and with accountability. I felt like I had no business being in a position of leadership and, in my deep shame, I quit my position effective immediately. Despite their pleadings, I was young and bull headed and just wanted to disappear.

I was grateful for the kindness and mercy I was being shown, but I wanted to just crawl under a rock and hide, and eventually I did. I left the only community I had known for the past few years and walked away from some of the greatest friends I ever had. God had pulled on my heart to keep me there, but pride and stubbornness were my downfall.

Six weeks later, I headed out to the front porch to check the mail and found a letter from my friend, Larry. I opened it up right there at the mailbox and read it. He wrote he hadn't heard from me in a while, and he couldn't figure out what had happened. He had asked a few friends about me, but he said, "The silence is deafening." Larry wanted me back in community. He didn't know what had happened and he wrote that didn't care what I had done. He told me it was dangerous for me to be out in this world alone. He wrote that I needed my friends to stand by me, no matter what the situation was or what kind of trouble I had seen. He told me he wanted me back.

I never answered Larry's letter. I didn't know what to say. I was too wrapped up in my own world to really give any serious thought to what he had told me. I kept the letter, though, for as long as I could. It's lost now, but might be buried deep somewhere in a place I still haven't found.

Larry died only a few years after we last spoke. In a horrible and tragic accident, Larry left us. I wasn't there, but some of the guys from our very first small group were with him until the end. The world needs men and women like my friend Larry, but frankly they are pretty hard to find. I think about him sometimes, especially when I see someone who looks like they aren't sure if they really belong. Larry was always quick to talk to those folks and bring them some kindness and the offer of friendship. He carried around love, compassion, and hope like people carry around a smartphone. It was always Larry's priority to love others, and he did it better than just about anyone else I've ever known.

I think, when we really are honest about this, we can understand that Larry truly knew me. He knew I was trying to handle all of this on my own, in some prideful way. I'd get a new job, right? I'd escape the looks and humiliation of it all, because that was the safe bet. I didn't need to drag everybody down into my problems, so it was better that I walked away, away from my friends and my church, wasn't it? Instead of staying, I acted like I was protecting them and ran away on my friends and the people who cared the most about me. These people wanted the opportunity to stand by me, but my shame and pride drove me away. I wished I would have let them be my friends.

Larry tried to model his life after Jesus. He knew everyone, no matter who they were or what they'd done, belonged in a tight community with people who would love them. Jesus was the perfect example of this. He encouraged his disciples to stay committed and close to each other, and most importantly, encouraged them to stay close to God. More than ever, and especially in the last week of his life, Jesus passionately lived and spoke about the importance of these relationships and the love we should show to each other.

Even during the times when Alice or I may have wanted to be left alone, God passionately desires for us to be part of a community of like-minded believers. Jesus held tightly to his own community, the disciples, and they stuck together and fought through many of life's most intense moments side by side. Jesus never gave up on them. Even when John ran away in fear, or when Peter denied him, or when Thomas doubted him, he still stood by their side and refused to let them go.

Sometimes we're alone because we are afraid that we may fail in a relationship. Sometimes we are alone because we've just been hurt too many times by too many people. Sometimes we're alone because life suddenly got really hard, really fast and we don't know what to do or who we can trust. It's like everything starts spinning out of control, so our days become more about our duties and what's required of us rather than about living with passion and loving and being loved by others. Sometimes we are just so devastated, as our expectations are completely smashed, and we just don't have a clue how to come back from something like this.

In chapter 16 of the Gospel of John, Jesus says, "Behold, the hour is coming, indeed it has come, when you will be scattered, each to his own home, and will leave me alone. Yet I am not alone, for the Father is with me. I have said these things to you, that in me you may have peace. In the world you will have tribulation. But take heart; I have overcome the world" (John 16:32-33).

An unimaginable darkness was on the horizon for Jesus and his disciples. Every word Jesus spoke to them was of the utmost urgency as their time with the Messiah was nearing the end. He knew what was coming, and sharing the specifics with the disciples would have yielded nothing but fear and pain. It was almost time for him to leave them, but not quite yet. They still had a lot to learn, and everything around them was about to become so much more intense. Maybe what they needed to hear most at that moment were these final words telling them "to take heart. I have overcome the world." As much as the disciples needed Jesus, they would soon have to rely on each other more and more. It would take sacrifice and friendship for them to follow God's path, and they were about to experience this in one amazing moment that none of them would ever forget. Jesus was about to do something for them, and it was all about friendship, sacrifice and humility.

I was exhausted and broken when friendship, sacrifice, and humility came in the form of my friend, the Alaskan, in April of 2009. He wasn't Jesus, but he was about to save me when my hope was almost gone and I was utterly spent. On a chilly morning in Columbus, Ohio, something pretty amazing happened to me, and when it did, I knew everything was about to change in my life. I would never be the same again.

Chapter 3

The Alaskan

"I am glad you are here with me. Here at the end of all things, Sam."

- Frodo Baggins from J.R.R. Tolkien's *The Lord of the Rings: The Return of the King (2003)*

The reality of my current physical state had set in, and that dream I had of sprinting across the finish line was all but gone. I felt the eyes of the crowd on me, mournfully gazing upon this broken shell of a human who didn't have enough left in him to run up one more hill. The sweat sticking onto my body for the past two hours now felt ice-cold, as the shivers had become pretty uncontrollable. My legs felt a deep heaviness, like they had been stuck in concrete for the past two miles. Even though there was only about a half mile left to run, my hopes were dashed and I was ready to give up. All I had wanted was to run this race to the end, but that wasn't going to happen today. In the end, my best efforts weren't going to be good enough, and it was time to give up and walk the rest of the way. My mind was made up; it was over. Not a thing in this world could have gotten me to run this whole race, until something happened I still can barely believe. Out of the corner of my eye, I heard yelling and then saw someone, and when I realized who it was, everything changed.

Six month earlier, I burst out my front door and started to run. My three hundred forty something pounds hustled down the street as I gasped for air while running on some suddenly very wobbly legs. My very breath was sucked right out of me! I suffered through half a block and thought – 'Holy cow don't die now!' No, I didn't die. In fact, this very moment on April 14th, 2009 might just be when I truly began to live. Watching a crazy looking, huge man run down their street was probably quite a sight to behold for my neighbors, but it didn't matter what anyone else thought of me anymore. I was just completely and utterly done with being obese. Three months later, I had lost a hundred pounds and a new life had begun. I was a runner.

We face rain storms, wind storms, snow storms, and even hail storms. Barking dogs chase us like we have raw meat hanging off the backs of our legs. The uneven roads and random construction and every other obstacle we encounter can feel like an endless maze drawn by a rambunctious four year old. One time, a guy threw a cup of ice out his car window at me. Actually, ice-chucking has happened to me twice. Is it a little stupid that I tried to chase the second one, he in his parents beat-up 1998 two-toned Dodge Caravan and me on foot? Maybe it made me feel a little better for the block I could see him still. If he had stopped, I probably would have turned around and started sprinting the other direction. Yes, bad drivers and randomly flung cups of ice are the worst, but it isn't all doom and gloom. Cutting just a few seconds off your time may be all it takes to put the biggest grin on your face. There is no greater feeling than completing a ten mile run as the sun rises in the East, while the moon sits quietly in the West. The long runs are exhausting and exhilarating. They can be painful and mentally taxing, yet they can feel so, so good. Your mind screams for you to quit, your joints ache, and your legs grow tired, but something in your heart tells you to keep going and take one more step. So, you do it.

In my forty-five years, I've experienced few moments more exhilarating than completing a long run. As much as I loved my new found freedom in running, however, I quickly learned I was never going to be very successful if I didn't start getting some really good advice. I needed support, encouragement, and the friendship of someone who could help me finish what had been started. There was a wealth of information and all kinds of opinions flying at me, and it all seemed to be important, but my brains were getting scrambled and I needed to discern what mattered most.

The aching feet, burning muscles in my legs, and those initial shocks to my breathing and body made for a brutally tough start, but only two weeks into my running journey I was able to run two miles without stopping. Can I just share that the smell of Ben-Gay was totally tolerable for me, but not-so-much for anyone else in the house? It left the grocery list quicker than it had landed on it! Back to the running, though, it was only two months later I could run five miles straight and had become very excited about where this new passion of mine had taken me. My confidence grew and I began to feel as if I were almost unstoppable. The beginning of my running journey was probably a little easier than you might think. Everything was going as I had planned, until I found out what my runner friends meant when they said they "hit the wall".

Hitting the wall for runners is the most dreaded of things. Basically, this is when you've gone as far as possible and you can't run a single step further. For me, my wall was anything over six miles; when I reached the six, my run was over. Sometimes my legs would feel either too heavy or go rubbery, like jelly, and I'd give up and start walking. Sometimes my mind would race with fear, I'd lose energy and would become completely psyched out. I couldn't seem to find a way to get past six miles. I endured failure after failure, and no matter what I tried, I wasn't able to reach my next goal. I kept trying though, and kept failing, and would have never gotten past those tough, six mile runs if I hadn't turned to the Alaskan.

My friend, the Alaskan, was an old friend and an experienced runner. After several failed attempts, it was time to make the decision to either stay satisfied at six miles or find someone to help me push through to the next level. He had once offered some advice when I first started running, and since the Alaskan had completed several half and full marathons, he had the experience to get me on the right track. I left him a voicemail and waited.

Almost immediately, the Alaskan called me back and we made plans to meet up the next Sunday. He took me on a six and a half mile run through his neighborhood. I wanted to walk after just a few miles, and finally on mile 4, just when we started going uphill, I gave up and walked. The Alaskan walked with me, but didn't let me off the hook and just a minute later got us running again. We didn't walk the rest of our first run together. When we finally finished, he let me know that next time we would run the whole way.

A few weeks later we ran the same course, and I was much more determined this time. The Alaskan and I stayed close together as we passed by the place where I quit running the previous time. He offered words of encouragement with each step, reminding me of my training and to trust myself. He stayed positive, no matter how much I was struggling. It was so tough to keep running, but I was out there fighting for each step now. As I pushed past the place I had started walking last time, I realized I was starting to run a little faster. My speed was picking up with each mile we ran and, before I knew where I was, the Alaskan told me there was only a quarter mile left.

He pointed to where we would finish off in the distance while I heard my friend say with all the enthusiasm he could muster, "We sprint now. Let's go!"

Gritting my teeth, my legs kicked high and hard and I was running as fast as I possibly could. There was no point in thinking about how far I had gone or the exhaustion I felt. I wasn't thinking about a thing other than going faster and faster until I couldn't find any more speed. Everything hurt and my breathing quickened as I just tried to hang on. But I *was* hanging on! My friend could have passed me anytime, but he didn't. He stayed right off of my right shoulder and kept pushing me to run faster. There was barely anything left in my tank, but I dipped my head, yelled, "Let's finish this!" and together we pulled off one final burst as we finished our run. I was exhausted and could barely breathe, but the high fives and shouts of triumph were the well earned reward of breaking through six miles, and I had done it with speed and strength.

Three months later, in October of 2009, my strength had once again left me and I was going to have to walk. After losing over a hundred pounds, I was now trying to finish the Columbus Half-Marathon, the first race I had ever run. I had only one goal, which was to never walk, not for one single step of those thirteen and one-tenth miles. I was on cloud nine the first ten miles, but reality started to set in and the next mile was simply horrific. Mile eleven looked like just one, unending hill set up to brutalize me. The chill of this frigid, October morning was settling deep in my bones, making everything so much worse. I had set out to run the entire race, but after fighting through mile eleven, and now just over halfway through mile twelve, I arrived at the bottom of a hill and stared at another long climb in front of me. I thought maybe I could run halfway up and then just walk as fast as I could to the top. Countless others all around me were now walking, so what would it matter? I could walk for a few minutes, make the last turn to the left, and then run the last tenth of the mile, which was mostly downhill. That wasn't so bad of a plan, was it?

I would finish the race, sure, but not on my terms. My dream had been to sprint across the finish line with my fist pumping wildly in the air as I achieved the iconic moment of my lifetime. Maybe my friends who supported me all of these months would understand, and maybe just being out here was enough. Each step was more than exhausting, it was painful, and my legs felt like they were coated in heavy cement. My lungs were burning and my body was covered in a freezing, wet sweat. No matter the efforts I was making, my hopes would be dashed, and nothing, not even the cheering crowd around me, was going to change this. I had done my best, and it would have to be enough. My biggest goal had been to finish this race without walking, but maybe it wasn't going to be my time after all. Maybe crossing the finish line would be enough. But as I thought about it, it didn't feel like it was enough.

Each new broken and tired step brought me closer to realizing running the entire Columbus Half-Marathon was slipping more and more out of my reach. My worn out body was almost halfway up the final hill and it was time to walk. This would be it. I was so close, but with nothing left in the tank, I was done. I didn't like it one bit, but this hill was too tough. There would be more races, of course, but this was my first, and it could have been perfect; it should have been perfect. There was nothing I could do, though. It was over.

Just as I had made up my mind, everything changed in an instant when I heard some very loud shouting that sounded like someone yelling my name. I looked over and there, with a huge grin, stood my friend, Dan Milam, cheering, waving, and clapping for me. Then, out of the corner of my eye I spotted a flash of someone in a blue cap moving fast out of the crowd, and I knew what was happening. I turned my head back around to face the last half of this hill in front of me, and my legs suddenly became light and powerful again. It was like a rebirth in front of hundreds of screaming spectators.

Seconds later, it was him, it was the Alaskan, in his blue cap, and he sprinted up next to me yelling at the top of his lungs, "C'mon Thad! Let's finish this!" Those words, the same words I had shouted three months earlier when he helped me break through those tough six miles.

In an ocean of twenty thousand runners, The Alaskan had found me. He had come back and rescued this wearied and tired runner who was standing on the brink of throwing in the towel. His race was long over and he had accomplished everything he had set out to accomplish for his personal goals. He knew, somehow he knew, that I would need some help to get to the finish line. Even though he had just run the same hard 13.1 miles, he was back here with me. I gritted my teeth, leaned forward, and surged quickly to the top of the hill. The crowd was going just insane around us, rejoicing in the Alaskan's shouts of encouragement to me. I was more determined than ever, and nothing was going to stop me now. My friend was here and he would help me finish.

We turned the corner and he told me one more time, "We sprint NOW! Let's go!"

I felt no pain or cold and was no longer tired. I was running as fast as I possibly could. It was still cold, and I knew I couldn't hold this speed forever, but my friend was with me and he wasn't going to let me down. As the finish line grew closer, my feet felt so light, like I was running on clouds. With the end of this incredible journey finally in my sights and with every ounce of strength left in me, I made one final sprint. Months of discipline and dedication had brought me to this amazing moment. It had been a brutal fight, but nothing could stop me. After all of the training, lack of sleep, changes in my eating habits, and all the miles under my feet, the end of this journey was now just a few feet away! I threw my hands up high and let out a yell as I crossed the finish line. It was over and I had done it! I finished the race with my friend and it was the stuff of dreams.

As I came to a stop, my mood quickly changed when a sudden chill swept through me. I was freezing and everything started to hurt. My legs were screaming and it seemed like it took forever for my breathing to slow down. A few minutes later, as we were heading home, Dan whipped the car off the road as nausea overtook me. I threw open the door and puked all over the side of the road. Throwing up was awesome, it was just so awesome, because almost instantly I regained some strength and felt so much better.

"You're a runner now," The Alaskan said with a grin as I shut the door.

"Right," I mumbled, still spitting some of the nastiness in my mouth out the open window.

Though there were thousands of runners on the course with me, it was the one who had sacrificed his own training destined to help me. My friend Jon Landis, The Alaskan, had found me and stayed with me as we ran up a hill and sprinted over the finish line together. He readily humbled himself and showed an incredible effort to encourage me to never give up. His personal sacrifice motivated me to follow him to the finish. He gave me a memory I would carry with me over many more finish lines in the future, all because my friend had stayed with me until the very end. In fact, he's crossed almost every finish line with me in my mind.

Much like my friend the Alaskan, Jesus took action, and by doing so, he showed the disciples his dedication to their lives. He wanted to show them that they were very important to him, and that finishing their race well mattered greatly.

"And let us run with endurance the race that is set before us, looking to Jesus, the founder and perfecter of our faith, who for the joy that was set before him endured the cross, despising the shame, and is seated at the right hand of the throne of God" (Hebrews 12:1a-2). In the King James Version, it says Jesus is the "finisher of our faith", which makes sense when you look at his life in conjunction with ours. God doesn't leave us to vex and wilt in the wind, rather he comes alongside us with the promises of his word and his actions and leads us to the finish. It isn't for our purpose or personal glory, but for the purpose and the glory of God.

In John 13, Jesus and his disciples are heading into the final days of his time with them and every moment is important. He specifically found and called each of these men to be his disciples just a few years earlier. They were some fishermen, a tax collector, and probably the most unlikely group of disciples anyone could come up with. For Jesus, however, they were perfect.

> Now before the Feast of the Passover, when
> Jesus knew that his hour had come to depart out
> of this world to the Father, having loved his own
> who were in the world, he loved them to the end.
> (He) rose from supper. He laid aside his outer
> garments, and taking a towel, tied it around his
> waist. Then he poured water into a basin and
> began to wash the disciples' feet and to wipe
> them with the towel that was wrapped around
> him. "Do you understand what I have done to
> you? You call me Teacher and Lord, and you are
> right, for so I am. If I then, your Lord and
> Teacher, have washed your feet, you also ought
> to wash one other's feet. For I have given you an
> example, that you also should do just as I have
> done to you" (John 13:1, 4, 12-15).

One by one, Jesus slowly worked his way among the disciples, washing their feet. It was a humbling moment for Jesus, as well as for his disciples. For years and years to come, the disciples would remember what Jesus had done for them on this quiet night. He humbled himself and did something only a servant was expected to do. These were no ordinary feet Jesus was washing, but the feet of men who had been travelling the hard and dusty roads of ancient Israel.

Difficult and dangerous days lay ahead for the disciples and their Messiah. As they looked to their leader, however, he was on bended knee washing their feet. As he sacrificed his position with them and humbled himself, Jesus showed them what was about to happen before the entire world. In that moment, he began to show what sacrifice truly is. He was demonstrating to the disciples that his actions in this moment were enough to make them clean. By washing the disciples' feet, Jesus was proving that he finishes the task in front of him, and this task modeled what Jesus was capable of doing with our sin. He took on the filthy and gross parts of us and cleaned them to make us more like him. He came alongside his disciples in the most important time of their lives and showed them his true nature and why he had come.

Jesus designed us to be part of something bigger than just what we see in front of us, just as he did with his disciples when he washed their feet. It was an iconic moment etched into the annals of history, this gentle humbling of a king who knelt down to serve his followers. It was an iconic moment in my life when he sent the Alaskan to help me sprint up a hill and across the finish line. It is found in the promise of Jesus when he told his friends, "I am with you always, to the end of the age" (Matthew 28:20).

I didn't need The Alaskan at mile two, but I needed him at mile twelve. To this day, I know I would have walked the last half mile if Jon hadn't dashed out of the crowd to come alongside me. As much as I had trained and as mentally strong as I had become, I still couldn't finish that race on my own. This is exactly why we need Jesus as the finisher of our faith. Jesus has been through everything, he sees everything, and he knows exactly what we need to finish this race well. Just knowing Jon was with me helped me get to the top of the hill, turn the corner and race across the finish line. Jesus, our champion, runs every step of the race with us, and he is the great finisher of every challenge we will ever face.

The memory of the finish of my first race encourages me and gives me strength when I'm out there alone on the long, tough runs. As I look at the medals and awards I've achieved, it brings me the joy and the confidence I need to go forward and keep running. The disciples now had a unique experience with Jesus and a powerful memory to look to as his time with them comes to an end. Every time the disciples looked at their feet, they could remember their sacrificial friend and go forward in confidence knowing he cared about them and was still with them.

The days of their journey together were coming to an end, but the disciples were full of memories of their time with Jesus. They could remember the way he healed the sick or fed the hungry. They were front and center when he addressed the hard-hearted religious leaders of his day. There were mighty and magnificent memories of the storms he calmed, or in his stories, those parables he told, about God the Father. They could think back to the time he walked away from thousands of people crowding around him for a vigorous climb into solitude, just so he could spend a few days alone praying on a mountaintop. He did all of this through his teachings, interactions with the people he encountered, and so much more. Jesus had been the disciple's role model, continuously building courage and strength in his beloved followers. More than anyone, Jesus understood how much these connections and moments together would impact their lives. As the end of his time on earth nears, his purpose became more and more clear, and his followers would then be ready. They didn't know what was about to happen, but whether or not they believed it, they would be prepared.

Everything was going just as the Father had planned.

Chapter 4

Prizes from the Cereal Box

"What makes authentic disciples is not visions, ecstasies, biblical mastery of chapter and verse, or spectacular success in the ministry, but a capacity for faithfulness. Buffeted by the fickle winds of failure, battered by their own unruly emotions, and bruised by rejection and ridicule, authentic disciples may have stumbled and frequently fallen, endured lapses and relapses, gotten handcuffed to the fleshpots and wandered into a far country. Yet, they kept coming back to Jesus."

- Brennan Manning, *The Ragamuffin Gospel*

If you were to ask me how many meals I consumed at Taco Bell between high school and college, I would guess somewhere between two to four gazillion. Is that a number? If it is, I'd say that's probably about perfect. My memories of Taco "Hell" run deep and long, like the time I took a first date there. Oh, we had just a lovely meal, surrounded by local high school kids and the employees that hated them, but the real fun began when we were getting ready to leave. I walked her to the car, and after opening the door for her (right now my mother is fist-bumping the next closest person while she is reading this), I then proceeded to walk around the car, open my door, and sit directly in the driver's seat.

As I put the key inside the ignition, I grimaced and said, "Hmmmm…I think my key is messed up. Why won't this stupid thing fit inside of my car?"

We sat in silent curiosity for a moment when suddenly…

"Wait! No! Your key won't fit because this isn't your car!" she screamed as she jumped out of the car faster than my stomach could react to the shock of the moment and the two bean burritos I just consumed.

My date and I survived this moment, though it may not be a big surprise this was our first and only date. She, obviously, wasn't up for a life of dates at Taco Bell and the kind of thrill a relationship with me would bring, and I was looking for a girl who can handle my unfortunate lack of car recognition issues. After this affair to remember, there would be zero dating for me for the rest of my senior year, and I'm quite sure she focused her time on guys who had more spending money and possessed a better memory of where they had just parked. This incredibly awkward moment, however, did nothing to taint my love for Taco Bell, and years later, when my friend Larry wanted to go grab a bite to eat, we naturally ended up at the Taco Bell parking lot in Schaumburg, Illinois, not far from the Woodfield Mall. It was the perfect place for a Mountain Dew and sketchy beef, and it's also where you go to get to the heart of it all with a good friend.

I'm sure there are many who could write more eloquently about the life of Larry Clarke, but I'm going to share another story of how he impacted mine. Larry wasn't married, most certainly wasn't pretentious or pious, and he hung around the church and its people all day, every day. Sometimes he was with close friends, of which he had too many to count, and other times he was out looking for lost souls and vagabonds, the kind of folks who needed a little love, hope, and Jesus. He had that small pension and lived a very different life, a life free of the monetary trappings of our western culture. He never claimed to be a theologian or great leader of men, but that's kind of who he was, at least in his own special way.

Larry connected deeply with all of us in our small group, and he was always our bright spot. I will forever treasure my moments with Larry for several reasons, but the conversation we had sitting on the trunk of my car in the parking lot of that Taco Bell will be the one that stays forged into my memory for the rest of my life.

That evening, our conversation ebbed and flowed from the guys in our group to how we were both doing spiritually. I was sharing about my time in God's word and started rambling about my personal devotions. I proudly shared with Larry how I was reading three chapters in the Bible every day, and how this was a huge key to my spiritual development. He paused and looked right at me, until I finally shut my yapper. Larry sat still, waiting for the moment he had my absolute, undivided attention.

Dipping his head down, eyes seemingly fixed directly into my soul, Larry quietly said, "I don't believe you need to read your Bible every single day, Thad."

What? Well, that was a weird thing to say! I immediately bristled as my face grew a little hot and my shoulders and lips tightened in irritation. I wondered if Larry knew how uncomfortable his words had made me. I bet he did! He sure kept staring at me, too! Raw feelings of defensiveness began to build quite quickly in me. I paused to look carefully at my friend, not having a clue how to respond. Those words seemed so bizarre and almost felt like some personal attack against me. *Were they?* I wondered. Maybe Larry was jealous because he wasn't reading as much as me. Maybe that was why he said that! But no, Larry wasn't the jealous type, actually, he was pretty much the exact opposite. I mean, here we sat, two good friends, and I had just expressed to Larry how important it was to read three chapters in the Bible every day. Shouldn't he be patting me on the back, leading the charge to declare me as some spiritual giant in the making? There had to be a reason why my friend said this.

The sound of some car's tires screeching out of the parking lot was the only sound I remember. I was absolutely and completely stunned into silence. Larry looked at me with a determined, yet compassionate smile and it felt like forever until we began to talk.

"You okay?" Larry softly asked, as he tilted his head and gave me a slight smile tinted with compassion.

We quietly began to talk, and then discussed, as well as slightly debated, the pros and cons of reading the Bible each day. I wasn't giving up, but Larry stayed calm and kind. That evening, in the Taco Bell parking lot, my friend walked me through the difference between a relationship with God based on duty and one based upon God's love. I hate to say I don't remember everything about that conversation, but I do remember he was firmly rooted in the prospects of God's love for us not being rooted in our actions. I was speaking to the urgency of soaking daily in the scriptures, but in my weak and legalistic mind, I saw myself as the defender of the importance of God's word in our daily lives. I was still missing the point.

I didn't walk away that night with any sudden epiphany. Honestly, for years the whole conversation threw me more than taught me. I missed what Larry was telling me until something happened to me, something to this day I can't even really explain.

"2013 is going to be the best year of our lives!" I proudly told my family as the ball dropped and we celebrated another new year.

I can tell you this – 2013 was undoubtedly the worst year of my life. In a matter of just a few short months, I went from being a respected leader in my home and my church, to suddenly living in a senior housing apartment with my seventy-six year old mother. I was suddenly broke and had legal and marital problems beyond my comprehension. Before I could catch my breath, I was thrown into a bizarre divorce and was absolutely desperate for God to rescue me from this whirlwind. Some of my friends described it as a dark and intense spiritual attack. Losses continued to mount almost daily, and my therapist was working to help me find even a little peace and relief.

It was a warm spring morning in 2013 as I sat in my car under a tree in a McDonald's parking lot in Wayne, Ohio. Sobbing my eyes out and crying out to God for just a little relief, he whispered softly to me of the promises of his love and the hope for a future. Yes, when I felt the most alone, he answered me. More than ever, his scriptures came alive in my heart and I clung to his word with what little strength I still possessed. Oh, those beautiful scriptures, clung to with white-knuckle by this broken man...

"God is our refuge and strength, a very present help in trouble. Therefore we will not fear though the earth gives way, though the mountains be moved into the heart of the sea" (Psalms 46:1-2).

"The Lord is my shepherd; I shall not want. He makes me lie down in green pastures. He leads me beside still waters. He restores my soul" (Psalms 23:1-3a).

As the Psalms began to connect with my soul, questions of what to do flooded my mind. There was still pain, so much pain searing through me, and I didn't know how to process any of it. False accusations and rumors flew around about me, and I was clueless how to defend myself. My brain spun a million miles a minute and I was tempted to scream to the world the injustice and wrongs done against me, but again, the Bible, God's words to us, rescued me.

"The Lord will fight for you, and you have only to be silent" (Exodus 14:14).

There was a deep silence in the darkness, yet a broken heart began to slowly heal. The losses of my marriage and several close friendships left me with so much pain, but God was filling those voids with the promises of his word. These scriptures, and so many others had become alive to me now, and they did so in my greatest moment of need.

The voices of men became less and less important, and my forged destiny by our Creator was made more clear every day. God wanted me to embrace and enjoy our relationship through his powerful love and good plans for my life. God wasn't interested in creating feelings of guilt and duty for a broken vessel of a man. He was embracing me in his overwhelming love, and God showed me he still had great plans for me. These words from the book of Jeremiah brought me a new hope, saying, "For I know the plans I have for you, declares the Lord, plans for welfare and not for evil, to give you a future and a hope." (Jeremiah 29:11).

Pride had blinded me to the whole point of that crucial conversation with Larry until those tragic days of 2013 struck. Because of God's love and rescue, I have never been the same. As I inhaled God's word, I began to exhale a new life, one very different than what I had before. It took me twenty years and the biggest pile of heartbreak and suffering to figure out what my friend Larry was trying to teach me. He was so very, very wise. He knew what to say and not say without breaking the spirit of a twenty-four year old kid. This wasn't a conversation about spending time in God's word. Larry was trying to eradicate the modern day Pharisee which was building slowly, but surely, in my heart. He loved me enough not to break me, but he knew to speak truth. He could see how I was in love with a number and the result of reading through the Bible in a year. Even though I was a follower of Jesus and seeking truth in his word, at the same time my Bible study had become very much about me and what I was doing. It took Larry mere moments to figure out my legalistic persuasion, and he brilliantly decided to love me in the best way he possibly could. Larry wanted me to be free.

In my heart I meant well, and Larry saw this, too. He was compassionate and smart enough to see I loved God and wanted to obey him. He understood and believed it was pertinent to my life to study the scriptures. Larry also was not blind to my desire to appear impressive and my desperate cry for some major lessons in humility. It would take experiencing the pain and hardships this life threw at me to help me understand the message of my friend. Larry died just a few years after we drove away from that Taco Bell parking lot. I will never be able to call my friend and tell him how wise and loving he was with me all those years ago. I am grateful for the love and grace of my brother who willingly cared so little about his own reputation and so much more about God's design.

In my time with Larry, he always showed a unique brand of courage because of his willingness to be told he was wrong and to appear as being spiritually weak. It was never a question of whether or not Larry valued the scriptures. We all knew he did. As a member of the small group he was in, I can attest to this, but loving God and embracing Jesus' love for me was more important than anything to Larry on this night. Larry didn't want me to elevate my personal goals or my own piety over my personal choice of loving God. He also didn't want me to be like the men Jesus addressed in Matthew 23, men who were captured by the status of religious accomplishments and power, and not by the amazing unconditional and all-encompassing passionate love of God.

These were the men who were always nearby, standing in the crowds, waiting to confront, harangue, and harass him. They wanted the world to see that no matter who he claimed to be, Jesus could never measure up. In Matthew 23, Jesus had watched these men called Pharisees and he addressed them. Jesus wasn't about to let these men coerce the crowds into idolizing perfection, he simply wanted them to see how God loved and adored them. While the Pharisees were about results and what could be obtained, Jesus was defiantly about the journey and the experiences of all of life, the highs *and* the lows.

Picture with me, for a moment, two nine year olds sitting next to each other at a breakfast table. They each have a box of Frankenberry cereal (the best!) in front of them, wafting out the delicious aroma of strawberry and marshmallow flavors. Suddenly, one of them lurches across the table, grabs the box, rips it open and plummets his hand in, grabbing for the prize in the bottom. What do you think the other kid is going to do? Will he sit there calmly, gently opening his box and pour this wonderful cereal perfectly into his bowl? Or will the temptation be just too much for him as he grabs the box of the beloved Frankenberry cereal, rips open the bag, spilling those glorious strawberry flavored marshmallows out all over the table as he too hastily pours it into his bowl?

The same concept holds true in our relationship with God. As we go through this life, too often we are caught desperately grabbing for the prize instead of embracing our many blessings in front of us. We also can catch ourselves looking around at others and comparing ourselves to what they are doing, and once we go down this path, we are certainly headed for trouble. The religious elite in Jerusalem spent their days comparing themselves to everyone else, and Jesus had plenty to say to them in response.

The Pharisees had strategically placed themselves in the middle of the religious and political mess of Jerusalem. Their persistence and devotion to prizes was almost unheralded. They clung to every opportunity they could find to elevate themselves above others and assert spiritual authority over them. The more they lifted themselves up, the more they pushed others to the bottom, or as Jesus himself described it in Matthew 23:4, "They tie up heavy burdens, hard to bear, and lay them on people's shoulders, but they themselves are not willing to move them with their finger." The Pharisees were often too busy making things worse for the second kid opening the cereal. They were the first kid, diving in for the prize, and rejoicing before everyone else in their newly found glory!

The Pharisees go on and on talking about opening the box and sticking their hand in and what they did to get the prize. Yet they didn't make the prize, put the prize in the box, make the cereal, make the bag, and they most certainly didn't come up with the idea of the prize. If you listened to them, though, they believed they were better than anyone else because they pulled out the prize, or even because they were able to sit in front of the cereal itself. They elevated themselves above everyone else because of their position and actions. Jesus, however, said, "They do all their deeds to be seen by others. For they make their phylacteries broad and their fringes long, and they love the place of honor at feasts and the best seats in the synagogues and greetings in the marketplace and being called rabbi by others" (Matthew 23:5-7).

By phylacteries and fringes, Jesus was referring to the ornate clothing the church leaders of his day wore throughout Jerusalem. In this passage, he was simply providing a visual illustration of the superficial measures the Pharisees clung to in their attempt to impress each other and everyone around them. Jesus was less than pleased with their drive for the right look and the right word. He was excited about those who loved God, enjoyed the journey and weren't consumed with themselves and their own desires.

I'm ashamed of the times I've read the Bible for selfish and vain reasons. I'm ashamed for when I've wanted to sound impressive or act like I know something special about God that maybe somebody else didn't know, and this all bothers me, and it should. The vanity and appearances of men and women clinging to their religious works is an ancient and tragic tale of a life wasted on all the wrong things. More than anything, I am grateful for all God has done and how he stayed by my side when I was a young man full of some bad ideas, and put people in my life to correct them, doing so in kindness and love.

Sometimes it takes us a couple of decades, some ugly sobbing, and that swirling nausea from the stress life mercilessly throws at us. I guess that's what it took for me in 2013 to rip off those blinders so I could see what God wanted to show me. And you know what? It's okay that it took me so long to understand what Larry was saying. You might say it was kind of like that awkward date at Taco Bell. When I kept trying to get my key to go into the ignition, I didn't even consider I was in the wrong car. It wasn't about being wrong, but about getting this right. It's why Larry was never heavy-handed with me, but took his time to show me grace and compassion. Sometimes we mean well, but sometimes it takes some pretty intense lessons from life for us to understand God's purpose in us. The disciple of Jesus doesn't walk an easy road where all the best plans all come to fruition. The disciple of Jesus faces great hardships and turmoil, and God then takes these tragedies and does something really good in us.

My dear friend opened this door for me, and many years later, after some pretty intense suffering, I walked through that door and found truth and peace on the other side. I found studying the scriptures is something far greater than some notch on my belt. I discovered they are the way God shows me his goodness and his love in my darkest moments. God's word isn't intended to be used as a means to prop ourselves up, but to understand him, to know him, and to see Jesus as he truly is.

One reoccurring theme within the Bible is that Jesus was known for showing kindness and love, especially in the way he approached the disciples and his closest friends.

It's why two women would soon come to Jesus in hope and faith to save their brother from a certain death. The story of Lazarus will soon be the biggest story out of Judea in years, and it will bring joy and cheering to crowds of onlookers. It will also be the moment where a murderous plot begins and where the history of the world will be changed forever.

Chapter 5

Alive

"And after you have suffered a little while,

the God of all grace,

who has called you to his eternal glory in Christ,

will himself restore, confirm, strengthen, and establish you."

- 1 Peter 5:10

"Zoloft," I muttered to myself.

With the bottle in my hand, the label staring back at me, I sat in my car in a place I'd never been before. How in the world did I get here? These pills weren't going to fix any of this, would they? There I waited, sitting outside of a therapist's office in a small suburb outside of Dayton, Ohio. But we know what happens here, don't we? I walk in, somebody shouts, "Let the healing begin!" and magically everything is okay. Right?

"The therapist will meet with you, Mr. Riley, but it needs to be in our main office where others are present. And it needs to be during daytime hours," they told me when I called to make the appointment the previous week.

Well, what was that supposed to mean? I wondered what my wife had told them when she met with the same therapist in this same office last week. Had she convinced her I was some monster, a twisted and sick man that people should be afraid of? Was the therapist concerned for her own safety, too? Maybe people would always be leery of me now. Maybe this was just the way things were going to be from now on. I slumped and exhaled deeply in what felt like another moment of defeat.

The clock on my dashboard said it was time. Tossing the bottle of Zoloft back in my center console, I shut the lid, leaned back in my seat and let out a heavy sigh. No, I wasn't going to take drugs. They wouldn't help me.

I checked my cheeks for any remnants of stained streams of tears and blew my nose one last time. Breathe. Just breathe. I opened my car door slowly and, with my head hung low, stepped out of my car.

It was just last week that I had started taking those pills in a vain attempt to help keep my emotions under control so I could function. Function. What does that even mean? Had it really gone this far? I guess it had. I needed to be able to work and to fulfill my day-to-day responsibilities without breaking into tears. I took half a pill every day, but it didn't seem to be helping, so after a few days I called it quits. Maybe walking into this little brown building would help me, but maybe it, too, wouldn't change a thing.

Suddenly, the back door swung open and a woman in dark sunglasses stepped through the doorway and towards her car. It seemed odd to wear sunglasses on a dreary day like this, but maybe she wanted to hide her eyes, too. I wondered if she was getting divorced or maybe her husband did something pretty horrible. Was there some dark secret in her past she had dealt with her whole life and finally decided it was time for some closure?

This door, this stupid, old, brown door stared at me, and once it was opened, there would be no going back. Deep, deep breath. My hand touched the knob and, before I could slow any of this down, I opened the door and walked into the lobby. I wasn't supposed to be here, was I? I mean, seriously, I looked around the lobby and there were only women waiting. Really, though, I guess there wasn't anything to lose anymore, was there? The older lady behind the window smoothly slid back the glass and I said, "Thad Riley. I'm here for a one o'clock appointment."

My face probably looked like a train wreck of tear stains and red eyes, but with a slight shift of her gaze to the calendar on her desk, she let me off the hook a little by attempting to avoid eye contact. It's not like it took a brain surgeon to deduce I had been crying only a few minutes earlier. Maybe the mirror in the car lied a little and maybe I didn't look as good as I thought I might. But she saw people like this all the time, right? She must have in this place.

She handed me a clipboard with that always dreaded stack of papers to fill out. You know, that ten stories high pile of former trees you get every time you go to a doctor or hospital for the first time. It didn't matter, though. I was just happy to be here and to begin this process of healing or whatever you call this sort of thing. Somehow being here would surely be enough to save my marriage and somehow teach me how to cope with everything that was happening. Right? Wouldn't it? Isn't that how all of this works?

To my surprise, and long before I was done with my mountain of paperwork, the door opened and a blonde haired lady with glasses and a warm smile called my name. I weakly smiled the best I could as she gestured for me to come to her.

"Come on in, Thad, and bring your mountain of paperwork with you. We can finish that up real quick in here."

Her warm greeting threw me off a little as she motioned to the couch on my left. I walked to it and slowly sat down. I thought we were supposed to meet somewhere public and wondered if maybe somebody else would need to sit in the room with us. She wasn't acting closed off or looking at me like I was a monster, rather she was smiling and friendly and definitely welcoming me into her office. Maybe this wouldn't be so bad after all, but we hadn't even begun to talk. Maybe she had an agenda and being pleasant early on was part of it. Was this how she would get me to confess to something I never did?

I *could* do that. I could just give up and throw in the towel. There were people who were waiting for me to offer some false confession, and I knew if I gave in they would talk to me about reconciliation and maybe this nightmare would finally end. They'd be excited to be part of a great story and the confession of a hideous man. It's not like they believed I was innocent anyway. I could go through some process of repentance and therapy and maybe get my life back, right? I wanted to spend time with my kids so much that I would do almost anything to see them. No matter how I sliced it, though, I just couldn't get over the cost. If I delivered a broken hearted and deeply sorrowful confession to things I never did, were there any guarantees I'd actually get my life back? And what if things got worse the next time? I kept thinking there would always be a next time, and it would always get worse. When I was quiet and prayerful and quoting the scriptures, like, "The Lord will fight for you, and you have only to be silent" (Exodus 14:14), God brought me peace and told me to be patient until he would pull me out of this fire. So I waited, no matter how painful it was.

The couch was a tight fit for me, just a tad lower than her chair. Like royalty sitting in a grand throne, she sat above me in her tall chair, and her glasses...I swear, it felt like those glasses saw right through my soul. Every word that came out of me would be turned over again and again in her mind until she was satisfied I was crazy, although she really wasn't acting like she wanted to tell me I was crazy. She smiled, and as I began to share some of my story, she nodded, seemingly in affirmation. She was acting like she wanted to be very kind to me, and for no real reason at all. The more she nodded the more I had to choke back the tears. I wasn't ready for her to treat me with respect and kindness, rather I had come in prepared for interrogation and disgust.

I was so tired and spent, I simply had no clue what to say, so I said everything. Her role in all of this was to help me, right? Or maybe she had already judged me, but had hid her intentions. She listened intently and had empathy all over her face, but maybe on the inside she was recoiling. After everything I'd been through, it wasn't like I had anything to lose, so running away wasn't going to help me or my children. I was here and, one way or another, I was going to have to get through this. I was in such deep emotional pain, and I felt so consumed by my personal losses. It was more than obvious I needed her help. This devastating tribulation had worn me thin, literally, as I was barely eating now. I didn't tell anyone there wasn't enough money for me to eat normally, just maybe only about a meal and a half a day. I got by, however, and learned how to ignore the hunger when I felt any, which wasn't often. My stomach was always upset from the stress, so it wasn't like I was jonesing to eat a whole pizza or anything. Being broke and feeling destroyed is by far the most effective diet plan I've ever done. Obviously, though, it's not so good for the soul. Working out almost two hours every day did give me a heck of a release, but it also made me question myself as I started to emphasize my worth in all the wrong areas. Determination and pain fueled those lonely, bitter workouts, but they also left me feeling kind of empty. Don't get me wrong, being physically healthy is important, especially in the tough times, but I was destroying myself, which is a recipe for only more pain and feelings of worthlessness.

She listened mostly that first time, somehow sifting through the rambling and broken thoughts of the exhausted and desperate man sitting before her. My brain was like a giant pile of confusing mush, but it slowed down every few minutes as I tried to figure out if my therapist actually believed my story. She sat there in her therapist chair, calmly listening and nodding. Somehow this approach had a calming effect on me. Maybe, though, she was a little skeptical of me, or was that just my imagination? She was intensely listening and taking notes, never giving me any concrete sign she didn't believe me. I guess since hardly anyone else believed in my innocence, I assumed my therapist wouldn't either. She gave absolutely no indication if she did or didn't believe me, only that she was listening and paying very careful attention to what I said.

Our time was up, and as I got up she thanked me for being open and vulnerable from the start. She seemed sincere, so that was pretty okay. There were a lot of questions, and though I didn't have all the answers, she thanked me for answering them the best that I could. Maybe my brain was playing a million tricks on me, but I felt like she could see straight through me.

I was doing a little better and felt a little more hopeful going into the next meeting, and she had even more questions for me this time. I still couldn't tell if she believed anything I said, but I had hoped she did. Inside of me began to swell this rare and powerful freedom as I didn't have to think about defending myself, and I really started to open up to her.

"It's like I can't catch my breath sometimes. There's this heaviness on me all the time and I can't shake it. It's like I'm…" I remember telling her.

"Bound up in chains?" she said, barely glancing up from her notepad when she said it, just enough to fix her eyes on me.

"Yes," I said with a giant exhale. "Bound up in chains is about right."

Leaning forward and looking intently at me she said, "Thad, 2 Chronicles 7:14 says, 'If my people who are called by my name humble themselves, and pray and seek my face and turn from their wicked ways, then I will hear from heaven and forgive their sin and heal their land.'"

"Why did you say that to me?" I asked, barely able to look at her.

Silence. She could see me fidgeting in the chair, and could probably tell I wanted to tell her something, but couldn't. Maybe I could try, though. My self-confidence and any sense of trusting others was so very wrecked, but she was different. My therapist seemed to believe me, and maybe trust started here. What did I have to lose?

"You're the second person to quote this exact same verse to me this week."

She was nodding and did that thing where I felt like she was reading my mind and just waiting for me to tell her what we both already knew. I could have done my best to figure it out, and lately I had been keeping my opinions to myself, but this time I felt like maybe I should say something.

"I guess God is trying to tell me something."

"Yes?" she replied.

With my head hung low, I half-whispered, "Maybe he wants me to repent of all of my sin and…"

"Maybe he wants you to experience his healing and his hope. Maybe he's telling you he will heal you and you can live in his light."

"I didn't hurt my wife."

"Then you don't need to repent of something you didn't do, do you?"

Suddenly, I lifted my head and a smile fell over my face as I fought back these awkward, little tears that began to form. Maybe she really did believe me. This was different, very different, from the counsel I had received from my elder. Instead of feeling overwhelmed, mistrusted, and constantly attacked, I suddenly felt validated and knew that I was still deeply valued and loved by God.

Sometimes after a session, she would give me an assignment to work on before our next meeting. Most of the time it would involve writing in my journal or other types of writing. Once, I wrote out a list of people I needed to forgive, specifically people who had hurt me yet never asked for forgiveness. She said it was going to bring me some freedom and peace, and when I was done, it gave me that plus something else – closure. The assignments were always relevant and often had a pretty big impact on my life, but there was this one...

"I want you to write a letter to yourself, Thad."

"Alright. A letter to myself."

"Right," my therapist said, "but I want you to write it as a letter from yourself today to yourself as a child."

A week later I walked into her office, and held out the letter and said, "Okay. I did it."

"Good. Why don't you read it?" she asked.

Dear kid,
You are loved. I saw this written on a sidewalk one time when I was out on a run. I was in the middle of the worst and most painful time we might ever see in our life and I saw these words written in the cement near an old house in a rough part of town. I knew it wasn't just for me to glance at and keep going. I knew the Lord wanted me to see them right in that moment. They changed my life. You are loved.
Kid, this is the beginning of your life and I have to tell you, much of it will be a fight, but these struggles will mean more than you can see right now. One day you will become strong, so strong you will be able to defend others and yourself, even in your most desperate days. You will have courage, because God will give it to you.

But this is not a fight where you will punch or kick or yell or say mean things back. Your biggest of all of your fights, my friend, is to show unconditional love and forgiveness to everyone, and especially those who have hurt you the most.

There is not always a reason why people are mean. Sometimes...a lot of times actually, they do it to make themselves feel better. The kids who do this are usually feeling pretty bad about who they are and how God made them. Sometimes it's because someone hurt or is hurting them. Maybe, when they come home from school, things are really bad. Really bad, and there's just no way to know if they are in the middle of something pretty horrible.

There could be many reasons people will hurt you, but those reasons are all bad and you won't ever find a good one. There will be days you need to stand up and tell them they're wrong and you won't be talked to this way. On other days you may need to just ignore them and keep wondering if anyone has EVER been this high on a swing before. Probably not, my friend. Keep swinging.

I have a secret for you. Can you keep a secret? I'm going to tell you something. I'm going to tell you something I think God wants you to know, but I want you to keep this a secret between us for now, ok? Ok! Your name is Thad, but you have another name and it's a name God calls you by. Your name is _____. That's right, _____. It is a name flowing with courage and strength and more than anything, love. You see, most specifically, God has given you a name and it's not about standing up and fighting, because too often we fight with our arms, right? No, my friend, you don't need to fight physically. You will have the kind of courage that can shake the nations and change the world. You, _____, have the courage to love no matter what. You do not live in the fear of being hurt or abused or ignored or rejected or slandered or called fat boy or anything that may happen to you. You have already been called Fat Boy, and it will happen again, but it didn't kill you when those boys called you that, did it? No, it didn't. And you will be called this name, and worse names, in the years to come.

You already know life will be tough, don't you. You are more ready for these things to happen to you than you know. You, my friend, will love others with the love God has loved you with. You will love with reckless abandon, and you will love those who will not be willing or able to love you back. You are not worried about protecting yourself, because you trust God to do that. Others will say you could get hurt or you will be abused, but I am telling you, you will be just fine. You will live a life of reckless love where you will become a beacon of grace and forgiveness and love to everyone you can who thinks they don't have a shot in this world. People will tell you to run, but you must rest in the truth that your power to love comes from God and you can sit in the heat until He saves you. And He will save you. The world will see defeat and despair, but they are blind to what God is telling you today. You are _____. You will risk everything to show God's love to a pretty unloveable world.

The devil hates you, and he will hate you more with each person you love. It's ok, he can't destroy you. But you may lose everything around you some day. You must be ready for the trials of life, and I know this is a lot to bear right now, but the devil can't stand for you to be out there loving the unloved and speaking about God's grace through Jesus. He will come after you. He will hit you where it will hurt the most. He will take things away and he will try to destroy your reputation. He will appear as an angel and then as the monster he is. Regardless, this is his game, but you don't have to deal with him. God will. You, my friend, will learn to trust God through the fires and you will find your strength when you need it most. God will protect you. I tell you this now and you must promise me never to forget it, but you must trust God. You will not be able to defend yourself. You must trust God.

You are loved. Start there and go forward in His grace. Tell the world and you will eventually become the man God made you to be. You are _____. You will find your courage and your strength.

Sincerely,

Yourself at age 42

You're probably wondering about the blanks in the letter, the place where that *name* goes. Well, we aren't there yet in this story, but I'll make you a deal. If you stay with me for the rest of this book, I'll guarantee you that you can figure out the *name*. Is that fair? Okay, and if you can't figure it out, email me and I'll help you. I know, I know this isn't supposed to be a mystery, but maybe you can give me this one. Okay?

"Was it the kids at school who called you Fat Boy?" she asked me after a few seconds of silence.

"Yes, but I had my moment of redemption. Let's just say that's a name that doesn't bother me so much anymore."

"Keep going," she responded not missing a beat.

"They always called me that, the kids in my grade school, junior high, and even my freshman year of high school. But I took that name back!" I said with a delightful grin.

"You took it back?"

"It was my senior year, and life was pretty good. I'd been lifting weights and was in far better shape, but I was still a pretty big kid. At lunchtime, my friends and I used to eat inside, but on the warm days we would walk around in our school's little courtyard. There was a group of guys, mostly athletes, who used to eat out there, and I guess they decided to have an arm wrestling tournament. So, it came down to this big wrestler against a basketball player, and after a tough match, the basketball player beat the wrestler and then jumped up on a picnic table and started yelling, 'I'm the champion! I'm the champion!'"

"I'm quietly standing there taking in the show, which seemed a little silly to me, when one of my dumb friends yelled, 'Hey! Thad just said he could beat you!' I turned around and told my friend to shut-up, but the guy on the picnic table yelled to me, 'Did you say that?' He looked angry and I guess he didn't want to be shown up, so I just shook my head and said, 'Naw. I never said that.' This guy was still standing on the picnic table and looking at me like he was still mad and yelled, 'Are you scared of me, Fat Boy?'"

My counselor stared at me as I continued,"Can I just tell you it seems like I've spent my whole life being called these names, and I guess I was finally sick of it. This kid was taunting me and I felt this intensity rise up in me, and it wasn't just about me. I was thinking about other kids he might say this to one day, and I wasn't having it. I looked up at the kid and said, 'Why don't you come down off your table and let's go.'"

"It was so quiet, and this kid was now awkwardly standing on the picnic table, and he just didn't know what to do. No one, I mean NO ONE, had ever seen me get mad before, but I was ticked off, completely and utterly. So, I sat down at the table, and this guy got some of his cockiness back, so he jumped down, sat across from me with his arm up on the table and said, 'Okay, Fat Boy, let's do this.'"

"He called you Fat Boy again?" she asked, not looking overly shocked, but understanding how fired up I was getting.

"Yeah. And so I put my arm up to his, and all of a sudden he's looking at me funny because my forearm was longer than his, and I suddenly realized I had all the leverage. Now I was smiling at this guy and he was looking concerned, and there was like fifty or - I don't know how many - students there. The wrestler he had just beat came over as we gripped our hands together and put his hands on ours. Well, the "I'm the champion" screamer kept squinting his eyes and his nostrils flared like some angry guy, and he called me Fat Boy a few more times as the wrestler guy gave the countdown and then shouted, 'Go!' He let go of our hands and, I promise you, it was like the whole world stopped for me."

"The whole world stopped?" she asked, with a slight smile on her lips.

"This guy, he was grunting and making these faces, and I'm just sitting there and, I promise you, I felt nothing. It was like I couldn't believe he was actually trying. It was like I was in another world and this yellow sun gave me powers and…"

"Superman?" she said with a little bit bigger smile.

"Well, yeah. Superman. So I said, 'Okay everybody. The Fat Boy wins in three! One, two and…'".

I paused, and she just looked at me. It was quiet, but it felt different this time. I mean, I had told a few others that story before, but I don't think it affected me the same way it did in the quiet office where I met my therapist every week. Maybe it was the letter I had written, or all the times somebody had called me Fat Boy, or those other names, those horrible names we don't write about in books like this. Whatever it was, this time was different. There were tears in my eyes and I didn't know why they were there. It didn't make any sense, but maybe I lied a little. Maybe those names don't ever really leave you. Maybe they always stay with you. She was waiting, though, for my story to end.

With those tears in my eyes and a quiet voice, I lifted my head and looked at her and said, "Three. I put his hand down so fast I couldn't even believe it. My friends went crazy and everyone else was kind of stunned. I stood up on the table and shouted, 'You can't beat the Fat Boy. The Fat Boy is the champion.'"

"How did that feel, Thad. Really, how did it make you feel?" she asked in a hushed tone.

"I didn't lose an arm wrestling match for over a year after that. No one could beat me. My forearm was too long. Kind of a funny thing, isn't it?"

She sat quietly and my head dropped again. No one had ever asked me that question before, but why would they? For everyone else, the answer was obvious, wasn't it? They knew I felt joy and elation and that I had just achieved some great victory in the face of a bully. But there was something unspoken here, something that needed to be said.

"I would have rather lost than have him call me that name," I said wiping my eyes.

"I know," she said, somehow keeping back the tears in hers. "I'm sorry."

"Yeah, me too. But it did feel good to beat him," I said with the tiniest of smiles and a chuckle you could barely hear.

"It most certainly did, I am sure," she said with a smile of her own. "And he deserved it. Have you forgiven him?"

"I guess I didn't think about it before, but no, probably not."

"Why don't we start with forgiving him, and then we can move forward to forgiving some others next week?"

A bigger smile crept over my lips as I said, "That would be awesome. Thank you."

For the next eighteen months, I saw her almost every week. It seemed like too often there was some bizarre and twisted tail to tell her, and everything was spinning completely out control for awhile. I had very good days, and very bad days. The bad days were a little more frequent early on, as were the good days at the end. But I was getting through life a little bit better each week, and at least I was starting to cry less, until finally, the tears completely stopped.

One of the most important lessons my therapist opened my eyes to was the need to take complete ownership of my own view of myself. I had put far too much value in other's words and actions towards me, especially those of my wife. Too often I would try to get her to love me, which caused her to resent me and me to lose more self esteem. For my own sake, I needed to stop placing so much of my value in the way everyone else viewed me.

She also taught me about boundaries and that it is okay to not allow people to have a position where they can destroy me. She encouraged me to guard the hearts of my children, and to help them continue forward with school, their friends, church, and sports just as they always had. I was learning about this new life and how to live as a single father, and how to let go of the abusive relationships around me in a healthy way.

Thanks to the boundaries I had put in place, I was no longer being judged or abused. I had begun to experience freedom and peace, and God's love for me was becoming more real each and every day. He was engaging me in new opportunities to serve him, and my strength began to return. The stress and pain were being very slowly replaced by wisdom and determination. I was able to look directly at God's word and make decisions for myself, without needing to feel like I had to get anyone else's approval. Having many counselors is a good thing, but there are times when people can be pretty controlling. I was learning to establish solid boundaries with those people, and the stronger I became, the less chance they had of crossing over those boundaries.

As I became more empowered, I was also able to address other areas of my life I had struggled through in my past. Confidence replaced uneasiness, and though I had recently felt so weak, a new strength emerged. The fruits of the spirit were becoming more alive than ever in my soul, and more than ever I was determined to honor God with my life, even if it meant standing up to some of the people I loved and respected the most. Eventually, I did just that, and I was so grateful for the chance to be part of reconciliation with them and to move forward in the goodness and grace of Jesus the Christ.

As painful as everything I had gone through was, the Lord used my therapist as part of the process for resurrecting my joy. My friend Misty Keener (née Laux), who knew me from many years ago wrote me during this process of healing that she believed the devil was trying to steal my joy. She said Satan wanted nothing more than to take the love and joy I have in Jesus and destroy it any way he could. And yes, the devil may have tried, but God had far greater plans for me. God inspired my therapist and some of my friends to rescue me, to be my beacon of hope. He encouraged me every day in new ways. Sometimes those ways were very small, but they were always very forceful and long term.

"When do you move to New Hampshire?" she asked me in the waning moments of our final appointment together. It was almost eighteen months to the day since I first sat down on that couch.

"In two weeks. Actually, we pull out of town on November 16th, which also happens to be my birthday."

"That sounds like a pretty good birthday present," my therapist said with a grin.

"My best ever."

"When is the wedding?"

"Basically, we go to the Town Hall when we get there," I said with giant grin.

Her small office got awkwardly quiet, maybe for the first time in all those months since we'd been meeting together. I didn't want our time to end, and I think she knew my deep gratefulness for her help getting me through this disaster that had only a year and a half ago been my life.

As we stood up, she looked kindly at me and said, "Well, let me give you a hug and you make sure you take care of yourself in New Hampshire!"

Not many people hug their therapist goodbye, but it just felt right. Once a confused, weak and almost destroyed man, I walked out through those doors eighteen months later with a new confidence and strength. Within my tragedy, I had grown in wisdom and love, and I was now about to marry the first girl I ever kissed who had become once again my most trusted friend. It was still hard to walk out the door, and it felt almost like it wasn't really happening, but it was. The saving grace was that I knew, no matter what happened, I would see my therapist again one day, either in this life or in eternity.

I look back on those early days a lot and try to remember everything I experienced and felt. I try to remember what it felt like to have my life and love ripped from me and to be brutalized emotionally by multiple people. It has helped me develop love and mercy, and it has taught me how to encourage others to trust God, even when it seems like everything is getting worse. I learned so much through the sorrow and agony, and I'm so much better for all of it. Most of all, I learned God will always love me and always take care of me. He resurrected the life of a beaten and weary man and brought me a new love and new purpose, and I am grateful for all of it every day.

You might be wondering why God allowed all of this to happen to me. Why didn't he just simply end the confusion and put a stop to all these horrible, ugly, and false accusations before they started? He knew my heart and he knew the truth, so why didn't that seem to matter? I remember the constant and sorrowful prayer of my soul in those early days, and how I was just so confused -

"God. If you're going to help me, what are you waiting for?"

But you and I both know this wasn't the first time someone had prayed that prayer, was it? I know I am not alone in questioning God this way. Even those closest to Jesus while he was with us here on earth questioned what he was waiting for.

If only Jesus had been there, he might have still been alive. Lazarus was dead, and there was nothing anyone could do about it anymore. They had gone to see Jesus several days ago, trusting him completely, knowing he could do something to save their friend and brother. Mary, the sister of Martha, was a follower of Jesus, and she knew he was the only hope of saving her brother. Jesus, well…Jesus waited. He actually waited two days before he left for Judea.

Between her sobs, Martha said to Jesus, "Lord, if you had been here, my brother would not have died" (John 11:21).

The Jews who had come with Mary were also weeping, and Jesus was deeply moved in his spirit. Yes, his spirit was greatly troubled. He felt the brokenness and heartache of his friends and their community who had lost someone close to them. Finally, mourning in the grief and brokenness of losing their friend, with tears and wailing spilling out all around him, "Jesus wept" (John 11:35) for his friend and for those who loved him.

Why? Why did he wait for two days? So much crying. So much brokenness. So many tears, even his own, and all because he waited and didn't rush to save Lazarus. This was Jesus! He could have called the fastest horse to himself and gotten there in time. Honestly, he could have called a giant eagle out of the skies above him to fly him to Judea. What good could come from losing a good man like Lazarus? Why did Jesus wait?

They had come desperately looking for help, but Jesus didn't race to save his friend, even though Lazarus was dying. After everything they had seen, Mary and Martha knew Jesus could heal their brother, and Jesus was close to Lazarus, so they knew he cared deeply for him. "So the sisters sent to him, saying, 'Lord, he whom you love is ill.' But when Jesus heard it he said, 'This illness does not lead to death. It is for the glory of God, so that the Son of God may be glorified through it" (John 11:3-4).

Whew! Everything is going to be ok, and Mary and Martha are most certainly relieved. Jesus, of course, clearly understands God's will here better than anyone else. In fact, it's God's will right now which rises above the will of anyone and everything else, including death.

Now, this is quite a statement to make of anyone, including Jesus. The good news is he isn't just making random statements without giving them much thought, and we know this because he clearly sets up his followers on this path several chapters earlier. As Jesus taught his followers about God the Father and himself, he also helped to provide perspective on this life and the importance of trusting God to not only guide us, but to take care of us.

John 6:38-40 might just be the entire setup for the story of Lazarus and what Jesus was facing. However, before we dig into this passage, we should understand how much tension there was surrounding Jesus and his ministry. At every turn, the Pharisees stayed close, hoping to catch Jesus off guard and prove him to be a false prophet. The political climate wasn't good for Jesus and his followers in Judea, in fact it was pretty downright horrible. The Pharisees had chased and harassed him, and they had worked to build fear and aggression into the communities where Jesus had been ministering.

"The disciples said to him, 'Rabbi, the Jews were just now seeking to stone you, and are you going there again?'" (John 11:8).

Jesus was taking a huge risk by going to Judea. His mission and ministry were critically important, not only to his followers and the people of Israel, but to all of us for all of eternity. It would have been easy for Jesus to take a pass and use the "Get out of Judea" free card he had just been handed. He was risking his life and everyone else's around him by going to Judea, but he knew what was going to happen, didn't he?

"For I have come down from heaven, not to do my own will but the will of him who sent me. And this is the will of him who sent me, that I should lose nothing of all that he has given me, but raise it up on the last day. For this is the will of my Father, that everyone who looks on the Son and believes in him should have eternal life, and I will raise him up on the last day" (John 6:38-40).

Something different was happening here, and no one else but Jesus knew. Jesus was ready, however, and although he waited two days before leaving, he went with purpose and faith. He was absolutely rock solid in his faithfulness to God the Father, and he knew what was about to happen with Lazarus. He was prepared for the journey to Judea, prepared to face anyone who would terrorize him and his followers, and he was prepared to fulfill his role as being the Messiah by defeating death. Jesus knew he could save Lazarus, and when he did, it changed everything.

The stone was rolled away and Jesus called to his friend, "Lazarus, come out!" (John 11:43).

"The man who had died came out, his hands and feet bound with linen strips, and his face wrapped with a cloth." (John 11:44).

Lazarus was alive! The tears of Mary, Jesus, and all of their friends were wiped away by a God who loved them, the great architect of their journey. Instead of mourning, a new excitement and joy filled Jesus and his followers as their faith in God was reaffirmed. Lazarus was a walking and talking testimony to the power of Jesus and his ability to defeat death. The whole community knew Lazarus had been dead and entombed for four days, yet now, because of Jesus, he was alive.

Jesus, along with his followers, had been healing the sick and diseased for a while, but in this literally life-giving moment, Jesus had publicly defeated death. If Jesus had come before Lazarus died, the disciples and Jesus' other followers would have never had this moment to lean on in the trials that were just over the horizon. This moment with Lazarus in the dangerous land of Judea not only establishes the love and compassion of Jesus, but also his power, energized by his passion, to do the will of the Father.

God wants us to engage in a life with complete trust in him and his plans. It probably felt impossibly overwhelming for the friends of Lazarus as Jesus stayed for two more days away from Judea after being told of Lazarus' pending death. God, however, had a much bigger plan, which was evident once Jesus had called Lazarus out of the tomb.

A new joy and a renewed faith filled the hearts of the friends and family of Lazarus. Yet, even as they celebrated, some of the witnesses ran to the Pharisees and told them everything they saw. Their reaction was filled with worry and fear, prompting them to create plans and a new agenda around Jesus.

"So the chief priests and the Pharisees gathered the council and said, 'What are we to do? For this man performs many signs. If we let him go on like this, everyone will believe in him, and the Romans will come and take away both our place and our nation'" (John 11:47-48).

The people have now been part of something amazing, and the truth of who Jesus was now resounded in all of Judea. The Pharisees were losing control, and they weren't asking God to help them understand what he was doing. They saw everything falling apart around them, and they continued down a path filled with darkness until they conjured plans influenced by pure evil itself. It wasn't just pride anymore, but something far worse. Fear and worry had driven them to something maybe they couldn't believe they were now going to be a part of.

"So from that day on they made plans to put (Jesus) to death" (John 11:53).

Chapter 6

My Precious

*"I have a great need for Christ: I have a great
Christ for my need."*

- Charles Spurgeon

She was being watched, but with all the people buzzing
around, she didn't really notice. In all of the pomp and
circumstance of the ancient temple of Jerusalem, the rich
were filing in first to drop stacks of money into the
offering. Her pulse quickened as she stepped into the
temple and quietly knelt down to pray. A group of men
were standing nearby boasting loudly, but this raggedy,
old woman didn't look like any of them. They were
dressed in their ornate tassels and finest robes while she
wore her old and tattered clothes. She had just wanted to
quietly go in and do what she was there to do. She was
poor and they were anything but. She was a widow who
was all alone in this world while they had their families,
friends, and status. She was the poor widow who came
into the temple in Luke 21:1-4.

We don't know much about who was there, but it was
likely a Who's Who of Jerusalem. Maybe there weren't
a lot of smug smiles and pats on the back, but even if it
wasn't as over-the-top as we might imagine, I wonder if
it didn't feel that way to her. Maybe I could be wrong
and it was a much more low key thing than I envision,
but I don't think I am. God always knows our hearts, and
he viewed this entire scene from a completely different
angle. Jesus looked directly at their hearts, their motives,
and he had a deep understanding of each person's

intentions as they dropped their money into the plate. There is no indication Jesus had ever encountered this woman before, yet he had knowledge of her life and experiences. His understanding went beyond what any other man or woman could see. As the Son of God, he was privy to all.

Our poor widow stepped forward and, in front of everyone, dropped in those infamous two coins. Someone was watching her, too, with a reverence and a deep love. Jesus! The face value of the money she gave on that day was ridiculously tiny compared to what others had given. Maybe there was a famous philanthropist gathering some serious attention. Maybe some royalty from a nearby country had journeyed with an entourage to drop off a massive amount of money and to make some new connections in the area. Maybe a local farmer had been religiously giving his ten percent for the past thirty years and he was just glad to get this over with for the week. Maybe the innkeeper didn't tithe that week because it just didn't make good financial sense to do it, but he would catch up pretty soon, at least that's what he told himself.

As the men in the temple were conducting business and revelling in this screwed up version of their own pious generosity, this widow has shown all of them what true sacrifice and worship looks like, and it wasn't on anyone's radar except for Jesus. You see, she didn't just give some of her money to God, but she gave all of her money, one hundred percent of everything she had to God. Yes, the poor widow blew them all away with her devotion and love and entrusted everything she had in this world to give a gift to the one, true God. How could men like the ones in the temple quantify what they'd just seen? They were so busy thinking about themselves that they couldn't see how this poor and simple woman was now towering in the greatness of her high position in the eyes of Jesus. Jesus didn't miss a beat, and he grabbed onto this moment as a lesson for his followers to learn from. Unfortunately, it's something many religious folks are still learning and relearning today.

I remember the time I flipped through what was on TV and caught one of those channels with the preachers sitting in purple and gold thrones. I was quickly drawn in and left it on for a few minutes to absorb the show, and quite a show it was. They jumped up, they laughed, and they hollered back and forth to each other, getting everyone riled up about what God would do if we called their 800 number and sent them money today. They spoke of these blessings we could receive if we gave, but it never sounded like anything Jesus had talked about.

Let's journey down the road for a moment with these folks sitting in these oversized purple and gold thrones. Some of these TV preachers who are asking for your money are making incredibly poor decisions with their finances even as I write this. One of them owns a twenty million dollar plane. When I heard about this story, I looked it up to see what his thoughts were, and he shared publicly he bought it so he could fly around the world to preach. He said it needed to be very fast so he could get to the places the Lord was leading him as quickly as possible. He raised the money through his very own congregation who gave it to him. I haven't bought a plane recently, but I'd bet my best Christmas cookie recipe you and I could find one for a good bit less than twenty million dollars.

When I saw those prosperity preachers on television for the first time, I thought it was a bunch of silliness and couldn't dream anyone ever really took them seriously, but there are millions out there who are hoping for a special blessing. I watched as this one man was swinging a prayer towel around and screaming and acting weird. He said that if we sent in a certain donation to him, he would send us a prayer towel, just like he had on his thirty minute program. This man with the wet, curly hair and overdone suit and tie said if I ordered this prayer towel today, my blessings would begin to flow in. All I had to do was send in some money for the towel, hold it when I prayed for big stuff, and then I would begin to be blessed in new ways, most of which, from what he said, would be financial.

At the same time, according to the website of the World Food Programs, about 3.1 million children die of starvation each year. This continues to be one of the biggest issues of our Western Civilization and in the rest of the world. While religious TV preachers are often caught up in the sales of prayer towels and raising money for private jets, people are dying all over the world and they need our help.

This is the world we live in today, and more specifically, this is a taste of some, definitely not all, but still some of the Christianity in America. We have prosperity preachers flying around in twenty million dollar private jets paid for by their very own congregations while children are dying of malnutrition all over the world. In other words, we are full of paradoxes and conundrums, with little change over the past few decades. In fact, things might actually be getting worse.

Knowing the world he lived in, as well as knowing what ours would be like today, Jesus had plenty to say on the matter. While Jesus spent his last remaining days in fellowship with his disciples, he went to the home of Simon, a man whom he had once healed of leprosy. They were sitting with the disciples and sharing a meal together. Suddenly, a woman walked in with a beautiful jar containing expensive perfume, and she began to pour it all over Jesus' head. Immediately, the disciples were disgusted and shocked by her actions.

"What a waste!" Judas Iscariot exclaimed. "It could have been sold for a high price and the money given to the poor."(John 12:5). If they would have thought back to some of his confrontations with the Pharisees, however, they would have known that Jesus could see their hearts and the motives behind their words. Don't think for a second that Jesus was going to drink Judas' bad batch of Kool-Aid.

The scripture doesn't share her entire story, but in John 12 and Luke 7 we come to understand that this woman with the expensive perfume was a sinner, someone Simon believed wasn't worthy to touch Jesus' feet. Whether or not she heard what the disciples were saying isn't told, but I'm not sure it would have mattered. The one who needed to hear the disciples most certainly did, and the only reaction in the room that counted was his. She may have been standing there defiantly looking at them, or just looking at Jesus with the loving eyes of someone who had found something precious. To her, that very personal sacrifice to Jesus made complete sense, and to Jesus, it was a crucial moment in preparing for what was about to happen.

As told in the Gospel of Mark, Jesus looked intently at the disciples and said, "Leave her alone. Why criticize her for doing such a good thing to me? You will always have the poor among you, but you will not always have me. She has done what she could has anointed my body for burial ahead of time. I tell you the truth, wherever the Good News is preached throughout the world, this

woman's deed will be remembered and discussed"
(Mark 14:6-7 NLT).

I have had a personal relationship with Jesus for about
forty years, yet I still say some of the most ignorant stuff
imaginable. So maybe before we belittle and write-off
the disciples, consider how you would have truly reacted
in such a moment. This woman was obviously driven by
devotion, commitment, and a love for Jesus beyond what
his closest followers could understand. She found
everything, including every ounce of her hope and
purpose, in him. It is also quite likely that she was too
wrapped up in the moment of being in the presence of
Jesus to pay any attention to the disciples. Even if she
heard them, Jesus spoke up for her quickly and
decisively.

The disciples had experienced first-hand the greed and
flamboyance of the temple and how power and
materialism corrupted so much of their world. Jesus
preached countless times about the urgency of helping
the poor, and the disciples were listening. What was the
issue here? What were the disciples missing?

Jesus was connected to the heart of this woman, and he
was with someone who loved him and found him to be
the most precious thing in this world. Jesus was more
precious than her expensive perfume. He was more
precious than her religious works. Maybe the most
shocking factor to understand here was that Jesus was
more important to this woman than her own reputation.
She was more willing to risk appearing foolish and
wasteful to a room full of men that she knew would
probably have something to say about her than to not
give everything she had to Jesus. In this one act of love,
she has become an iconic figure for all of eternity. And

Jesus was right; over two thousand years later we are still talking about her.

"My precious." It is one of the most famous lines from one of the most iconic characters in the history of cinema and writing. The creature Gollum, from the books and movies *The Lord of the Rings*, had been obsessed for over five hundred years with the Ring of Power. He was so attached to the ring that it changed his perspective on life, love, and friendship. He killed his best friend for it. He ran deep into the dark caverns of a mountain to hide from anyone who might steal his "precious". Everything about the ring consumed Gollum, even to the point of transforming him. It changed the way he looked and also how he saw everything around him. Anything different in the small sphere of his world made him wrought with fear, causing him to act out in some vile ways. His entire mission in life was to protect just one small possession which had given him feelings of power and completeness. He had no true friends, no family, and no purpose. The ring was his main identity and source of contentment in his world.

Frodo Baggins, a hobbit of quite pure intentions, was probably the one true friend Gollum had. By the end of the book and movie, the ring had corrupted Gollum to the point of attempting to kill his only friend, and he almost succeeded a couple of times. Frodo's best friend, another hobbit by the name of Samwise Gamgee, remained Frodo's friend despite the temptations of the Ring of Power. Even when Sam possessed the ring, it did not change who he was. Sam's friendship with Frodo was more precious to him than the ring, and his duty was to serve his friend to the very end.

In the end, the One Ring destroyed Gollum. What he treasured above everything else in this world was eventually the same thing that took his life. Some have their own "rings" today, and refuse to believe anything could be more important than their "precious". As Gollum worshipped his "precious", many Americans are worshipping sex, greed and materialism, careers, social status, their reputations, false doctrines and religions, and even our very own selves.

Worshiping Jesus, valuing him above everything this world has to offer, is a completely different type of worship. In Matthew 2:11, the wise men "saw the child with Mary his mother, and they fell down and worshipped him." When Simeon, a righteous and devout man in Jerusalem, first encountered the baby Jesus, "he took him up in his arms and blessed God and said, 'Lord, now you are letting your servant depart in peace, according to your word; for my eyes have seen your salvation that you have prepared in the presence of all peoples, a light for revelation to the Gentiles, and for glory to your people Israel'" (Luke 2:28-32). Even when Jesus was an infant, he created a profound worship experience for those he came in contact with, including powerful and respected men of this time. As we will see in the chapters ahead, Jesus was worshipped, to be found precious, by people from all walks of life. This narrative continues today.

It was the Summer of 2013 and I was pulling into the parking spot outside of my mom's condo. I had been living there on and off for several months, but this time was just after the police had served me with the Domestic Order of Protection. As I parked, the first text came in, and then another, and then a message from an old friend I hadn't seen in years. They were about a minute apart, and they each said basically the same thing. Something had been posted publicly on social media about me, something pretty horrible.

While scrolling through the post, deep feelings of exhaustion and hopelessness moved through me as I exhaled loudly. Although it was a bit strange, anyone reading this would come to one conclusion about me - I was a monster. There were no names, no specifics, but there were no vague innuendos either. Anyone who had questions about why I was living with my mom, was unable to go home, and couldn't see my kids very often would now understood why.

Years ago on a long drive, I was flipping through the dials on the radio and I came across a talk show. They were interviewing a psychologist who said that "men desire respect more than anything else in this world," and it surprised me, but now I think that makes sense. In this one moment of enduring the public shame of a brutal social media post against me, any hopes of keeping secret the pain, agony, and confusion swirling around me were over. I was a monster, and my scarlet letter carried a heaviness I had never imagined.

The Lord had shown me through his word that I needed to be silent and to allow all of these things to happen to me without response. Through Joseph and the story of Potiphar's wife, we see how God so often works for our good. Horrendous and false accusations were made against Joseph, but he never sought revenge or tried to fight against those who hurt him. Joseph moved forward in a spirit of optimism and continued to do the work of the Lord. I was, and still am, incredibly grateful for the story of Joseph and how God put this story there so we can know how to give everything over to him, including our reputations. God impressed on my heart the urgency of my own obedience, and he specifically led me to be silent and to not respond to any allegations. My reputation was precious, and I despised the thought of now being known as some two-faced monster who had lived a life inflicting violence and abuse on those I was supposed to love the most. God, however, had been clear, so I laid any hopes of gaining back the respect of men at his feet and waited for him to heal me from this nightmare.

As precious as my reputation may have been, God showed me that obedience and being faithful to him was more precious. As I leaned on him, the promises in his word assured me that trusting him in times of trouble was precious. When a few family members told me to defend myself and I didn't, they thought I was off my rocker, and they had no scruples about telling me so. They didn't understand that my reputation had become less precious to me than following God. I didn't blame them, though. I didn't blame them a bit, because as we see in Luke 7 and Mark 14, there was a time when even the closest followers of Jesus were confused about what was the most precious.

In Luke 7:36-50, the rest of this woman's story comes to light. Not only did she anoint Jesus' head in front of a minimum of thirteen men, she also washed his feet with her tears and wiped them with her hair, and then poured the expensive perfume all over his feet! In any society, this would likely be viewed as wasteful and possibly bizarre, but Jesus knew these actions were inspired by his Heavenly Father to prepare him for the task ahead of him. This special anointing for his burial deeply moved Jesus, but, with the help of God's inspiration, we can understand how those around Jesus struggled with his value and how the world perceives worth.

The disciples loved Jesus and were willing to give up their lives to follow him. This woman also loved Jesus, but she was willing to give up not just her physical life, but her reputation and all of her ideals to follow him. His disciples questioned Jesus about the appropriateness of her actions simply because she demonstrated how she valued Jesus far above anything or anyone else.

She poured valuable perfume on Jesus. She poured her reputation on Jesus. She poured out her anxiety of what the people in that packed out house thought of her on Jesus. No one else needed to approve or understand; Jesus did. Just Jesus.

In her actions, we see that nothing else could compare to Jesus, including how she was viewed by others. We see this often today in our culture as we struggle to understand others' deep commitments to Jesus versus the cultural norms. If we are truly going to impact the world and make a difference, we have to begin at a place of humility and a place where we value Jesus far above anything else. Jesus is more important than our ideals or our reputation surrounding our commitment to our ideals. Too often, we as Christians today are worshiping our ideals more than we worship Jesus. Attached to this is the risk of loving our own reputations and identities within those ideals more than we love Jesus. Ideals and reputations are never as important as Jesus.

America has moved into a time of flying rhetoric, never more on display than in the 2016 Presidential Election. Candidates pretty much said everything they could to get elected, all while establishing their candidacies to their base and their core group of campaign workers. The campaign workers diligently marketed their chosen candidate and, if they are good at what they do, they fulfilled all of their duties to convince others to make the same choice. Oftentimes in elections, those duties and responsibilities are what makes a campaign worker effective and helps put the candidate in the best possible position to be elected. Their passion, though, is often short lived because even the most passionate causes can eventually fade away from our hearts. Jesus, however, is eternal and with him comes an eternal relationship and reward, which is such a unique idea, it's difficult for us to truly understand. The love of God is all encompassing, and you can discover it most often through the promises of his word and the encouragement he brings.

God knows everything about us, including the motives of our hearts. He sees everything and knows where our passions truly lie. The woman in this passage placed her worship of Jesus far above any criticism she might have received, the potential anxiety of losing something expensive, and above her own personal desire to be beautiful. In the deepest parts of her heart, she considered Jesus precious and valuable above everything else and was willing to be ridiculed by a group of men because of her actions.

Our society, and this includes Western Christianity, too often honors the works over the heart. Motives are not easy to figure out, and we have to trust our brothers and sisters as they serve God. Most importantly, the question we must ask ourselves is simply this – what is most precious to us? Is the love and life of Jesus Christ most precious? Are the ideals surrounding our religious beliefs most precious? What is truly the most precious and how does it affect our worldview?

The worldview of so many has been skewed by what they deem as most precious. Whether it's a Ring of Power, our money and possessions, or our reputation, none of these things will ever be part of our eternity. Nothing else would or could provide us with what we need most in this life --- salvation. Jesus is the most precious because he provides salvation, peace, and his actions demonstrated his deep love for us. Only Jesus has the power and the deep love to give such a precious gift to you. Only Jesus.

There is someone else, though, and he will do anything he can to prevent you from discovering that Jesus is truly what is most precious in this world. He will use every ounce of power he has to lead the world down a path of destruction and chaos, yet to the world, it looks like the wide and easy path. His agenda is clear, and his methods are ruthless. As Jesus stands as your ultimate hero, this evil one is your ultimate detractor, and is hell-bent on your destruction.

His name is the devil, and he hates you.

Chapter 7

Devil

Don't think of Satan as a harmless cartoon character with a red suit and a pitchfork. He is very clever and powerful, and his unchanging purpose is to defeat God's plans at every turn— including His plans for your life.

- Billy Graham, in The Journey

"Be sober-minded; be watchful. Your adversary the devil prowls around like a roaring lion, seeking someone to devour" (1 Peter 5:8).

Rainbow Forest Baptist Church's annual picnic was filled with all of the glorious things I hoped to see at a church picnic. Burgers and hot dogs sizzled on the grill, families and friends were throwing bean bags through a hole and playing all kinds of other yard games, and there was even a bounce house for the little kids to go crazy in, and boy did they go crazy. But has anyone actually seen a bounce house where little kids don't act crazy? I spent my time in the thick of it, strolling through the church parking lot, enjoying the view of my kids playing, joking around with my friends.

The bounce house drew all the little kids' attention, including my youngest girl, just three years old at the time, and she would absolutely not be denied. As fun as my girl is, she has always been a bit more cautious than some of the others, especially some of those rowdy boys, but she was having a blast in there, flying from side to side with the greatest of ease. I was about ten feet away, casually talking with my friend, the Fire Chaplain, Richard Lipes.

It was the fall of 2008, roughly six months before I began my weight loss journey. My scale probably had me anywhere from three hundred forty to three hundred eighty pounds. The world feels different when you're that heavy. You often feel huge and slow, sure, but you are also powerful because you've got some leverage due to your extreme weight. That's kind of how I felt. I felt pretty strong.

What happened next still freaks me out to this day! Richard and I were calmly talking when all of a sudden, out of nowhere, I felt a powerful force propel me forward. For a split second, I thought maybe this could be a friend of mine kidding around, but I quickly realized none of my friends, and no human I've ever known, could have moved me so rapidly and with such undeniable force. No man, no matter how strong, could have come behind and shoved me forward in such a forceful way.

Life slowed to an almost complete halt, like I was Keanu Reeves in the movie *The Matrix* and dodging bullets, but I wasn't dodging a thing. It took my knees buckling and my falling back onto the hood of the car to realize what was happening. My feet were being pulled under its front end and time felt frozen as I could hear bystanders screaming in horror for the driver to stop. After about ten feet, she finally did.

I lurched forward off of the front hood and tumbled onto the ground in front of the car. My friends rushed to me, along with a doctor and a nurse who, by chance, were also at the picnic. Wiping the gravel off my face and in complete shock, I just laid there trying to figure out if I was okay. The doctor said things, but they were a blur. I ended up sitting up while he examined me. Everyone, including me, was beyond shocked I didn't have a single scratch on me.

I think they told me she was in her nineties? Our Pastor, the sweetest and maybe best man you might ever meet, Dr. Michael Grooms, was calmly speaking with the lady, trying to understand what had just happened, while also making sure she was able to control her vehicle properly. She ended up getting a ride home, and I don't know if she ever drove again, but it was probably best if she didn't. There was no sun blinding her or any other obstacle in her way. I was standing in the middle of the path her car was on when she hit me.

The whole thing was just so bizarre. I had just been hit by a car in front of a bounce house of about thirty little kids. If I hadn't been there, she would have driven just a little further and would have hit one, if not many, of the children. Honestly, I think we were all in such shock that I wasn't hurt that we didn't have much of a chance to think about all the little kids running around at first. And then, it started to sink in. A chill swept through me as I sat there on the ground watching them play, completely oblivious to what could have happened to any one of them. My friends starting looking back and forth between me and the bounce house, shaking their heads and putting their hands over their mouths. I don't think any of us wanted to say what we had all started thinking.

The overwhelming force, though, haunted me. The power of a car hitting me was unlike anything I had experienced. Not knowing what it was for a brief second and just being forced forward was terrifying at best. I had never felt anything like it in all of my life. Such an absolute and unbelievable force propelling me in a direction I absolutely did not want to go, and there was nothing at all I could do to stop it. If it had been a human, there would have been something I could have done to at least adjust to the force, avoid it, or even try to slow it down. I was completely helpless to do anything but just stand there and get hit by that car.

The rogue driver wasn't my enemy and she obviously wasn't trying to fill me with terror, but she did. Overwhelmed. Powerless. Afraid. In a matter of seconds, a lady close to ninety years old was able to make me feel all of these things, and she didn't even try to do it.

Overwhelmed. Powerless. Afraid. Six thousand years ago a man named Job experienced the same feelings, and even more so intensely. Job's story was different, however, because there was a specific enemy who had targeted Job and had set out to destroy him in whatever way he possibly could. The force I felt from the car was something I'll never forget, but I wasn't dealing with a powerful and evil spiritual being trying to destroy me.

In just a few devastating and heartbreaking moments, Job experienced some of the deepest losses imaginable. First, he lost all the animals on his farm, and then almost all of his servants were killed either by an accident or his enemies. Just moments later, he received news that a great wind came in and tore his children's house down, killing his seven sons and three daughters. A broken and distraught Job shaved his head, tore his clothes, and fell to the ground mourning all of his deep and agonizing losses.

This wasn't bad luck. There was nothing random about those catastrophes. We can't shrug our shoulders and just say, "Life is hard." It had all been someone's evil plan. Someone filled with such an intense hate and a raw desire for destruction that he would stop at nothing to destroy Job.

> Now there was a day when the sons of God came to present themselves before the Lord, and Satan also came among them. The Lord said to Satan, "From where have you come?" Satan answered the Lord and said, "From going to and fro on the earth, and from walking up and down on it." And the Lord said to Satan, "Have you considered my servant Job, that there is none like him on the earth, a blameless and upright man, who fears God and turns away from evil?" Then Satan answered the Lord and said, "Does Job fear God for no reason? Have you not put a hedge around him and his house and all that he has, on every side? You have blessed the work of his hands, and his possessions have increased in the land. But stretch out your hand and touch all that he has, and he will curse you to your face." And the Lord said to Satan, "Behold, all that he has is in your hand. Only against him do not stretch out your hand" (Job 1:6-12a).

All of those tragedies in Job's life had been orchestrated and executed by the devil himself, Satan. Once the most beautiful and powerful of all of the angels, he had wanted power for himself and chose to oppose God at all costs, even to his own demise. All evil, sin, hate, murder, despair, addiction, racism, and abuse began when Satan left heaven, cast to the earth with a third of the angels, now-turned demons. Those demons joined ranks with Satan and became part of his force of evil in this world. If this series of attacks weren't gut-wrenching enough, the confusion it created around Job's friends, shockingly enough, actually made it worse.

Job was disassociated from his friends because of the intensity of the tribulations he had endured. None of Job's friends understood why this had happened, and I guess they felt he needed to be able to explain. If there was no logical explanation, then horrible things could happen to anyone, even them, right? No, for them there had to be a reason why. At first, Job's friends mourned with him, but they quickly repositioned themselves as some of Job's biggest antagonists. Again and again they tried to find reasons to blame Job for his colossal losses, and again and again they came up with nothing. Maybe they were more comfortable believing something like that could never happen to them. If Job didn't deserve everything, what did that mean? Could they, too, face great suffering and attacks?

With his friends trying to attach the blame for all of this on him, Job was left alone to wallow in his grief. They may have been in the vicinity, but they clearly weren't showing sympathy or love to their friend in his deepest agony. While Job's friends were probing into his life trying to somehow explain the nightmare away, Job felt more isolated by the moment. He was not only alone in his grief, but also had to debate with his friends endlessly about the source of his loses. Heartbroken and exhausted, Job wanted to give up.

Alone. By separating us from our friends and church, the devil has a greater chance to attack us, which was exactly what he did to me. With the intense circumstances surrounding my divorce and the whirlwind around me, I spent much of 2013 on my own. During that time, the devil's attacks were often ruthless and cunning. The enemy would first remind me of my many failures. He would tell me I wasn't a very good father and feed me lies that I deserved all of this. He would then harass me endlessly about any mistake I made or sin I committed or just for being who I am in this world, which caused me to further detach myself from more and more friends.

I stopped calling or reaching out to others, save a select few. I left all forms of social media and let messages go unanswered for longer than was polite. More than ever, I was convinced I had failed God, my family, and my friends, which was in line with what a few people had been telling me. I didn't know how to defend or define myself, so I just disappeared. If you know anything about me, it's pretty impossible for me to disappear, but it was the only option that made any sense at the time.

I wore hoodies in public to hide. I walked with my head down, hung to the ground, defeated and broken. I would go to dinner alone almost every night. I'd sit on the second floor of this Mexican restaurant and eat and write and write and write. Sometimes I'd talk a little to my waitress, but mostly I was quietly talking to God while somberly taking in my new world all around me. I'd look down and see them below in the shopping center, all of these men who seemed so happy and fulfilled, while I sat alone in a whirlwind of confusion and pain. I am convinced the devil wanted to use every moment I spent alone to confuse, isolate, and hurt me even more, just like he did to Job. He wanted to play on my doubts and convince me I had done something to deserve all of this. The more I believed his lies, the more I removed myself from everyone else and became more and more vulnerable to his attacks.

"So weak."

"So sinful."

"They'll never believe you, and they will never respect you."

"Your name will always remind them of people who are not who they say they are."

"No one believes you. They think you deserve all of this."

"You'll never get your old life back."

"It's over. The life you once had is gone."

Like a wildfire, these thoughts consumed me. It often felt like I couldn't control them or stop them. It was an onslaught of discouragement and lies, and I'll always believe it came from the devil himself. Those words had a purpose, attempting to isolate and break me in ways I never dreamed of. I felt destroyed, attacked, labeled, and I didn't know how to clear my name and reclaim my life. Darkness settled in all around me, and the enemy proved to be cunning, determined and destructive. What little hope I clung to was only in God, which was exactly where the Lord was waiting for me. Jesus, however, was no stranger to confrontations with Satan, and he was there for me with hope and the promise that he has already defeated the devil.

"Then Satan entered into Judas called Iscariot, who was of the number of the twelve. He went away and conferred with the chief priests and officers how he might betray (Jesus) to them. And they were glad, and agreed to give him money" (Luke 22:3-4).

Judas Iscariot began his journey down a path leading to infamy as his plans started to unfold for the betrayal of

Jesus Christ. Whoever Judas may have once been, or who the other disciples thought he was, that person was no more. Judas was now possessed, literally, by the devil himself, and in all of his pride and arrogance, he showed up for the Last Supper of Jesus Christ. All the disciples were there for that final meal and time together. The ministry of Jesus had often involved sitting together for a meal, but those experiences weren't always times of reflection, peace, and a deeper connection to each other. They had had some precarious dinners before, like in the homes of tax collectors and Pharisees, but there was nothing like that last one. No one, except Jesus, knew the devil was at the table, and there was no telling what would have happened if the disciples knew Satan was right there drinking from the same cup they had to their mouths.

> When it was evening, he reclined at table with the twelve. And as they were eating, (Jesus) said, "Truly, I say to you, one of you will betray me." And they were very sorrowful and began to say to him one after the other, "Is it I, Lord?" He answered, "He who has dipped his hand in the dish with me will betray me." Judas, who would betray him, answered, "Is it I, Rabbi?" (Jesus) said to him, "You have said so" (Matthew 26:20-23,25).

Jesus looked Judas in the eye as he identified his betrayer. There was no fear in Jesus when confronting the devil, only a deep resolve and a purposeful determination to fulfill God's plans that would forever be unmatched in the history of the world. There were more pressing things on Jesus' mind right then. Those were his last moments with his disciples before his death, and he wasn't going to let anyone, including Satan himself, destroy that time together.

Jesus passionately loved his disciples, and he loves us just the same. He refused to back down to fear and confusion, or to retreat into protection tactics. Jesus wasn't planning or hiding, but experiencing communion, breaking bread and showing his disciples what it looked like to obey God and to love his people. He was not thwarted by Satan's presence one bit. In fact, we've seen this once before, haven't we?

"Then Jesus was led by the Spirit into the wilderness to be tempted there by the devil. And after fasting forty days and forty nights, he was hungry. And the tempter came and said to him, 'If you are the son of God, command these stones to become loaves of bread'" (Matthew 4:1-3).

In that moment, Jesus was in desperate need of food, and the devil offered relief for his intense hunger. Jesus, just like Job, stood alone against the devil. The devil's mission was to attack Jesus at his weakest point, when he was the most desolate. He similarly waits for us to be isolated, or influences our circumstances to get us away from anyone who might help us, and then ruthlessly goes on the attack. He hits you at your lowest point and does so in such an overwhelming way that you feel defenseless, just like I felt when I was hit by the car.

If you ever begin to lose sight of God's love for you, take a look back at the Last Supper and see what great strength of love he truly possesses. Jesus was direct and honest, and more than anything, he honored God. The journey Jesus and his disciples were on was about to change greatly, and the disciples would need this memory to go forward in their future ministries. They would need to remember how Jesus observed the Passover and had supper with them. They would need to remember Jesus still did that despite the madness and confusion swirling all around him. They would definitely need to remember that Jesus was not afraid of anyone, or of his future, no matter how hard that road was about to become.

We have the highest standard, and this standard is set by Jesus himself who underwent a far worse betrayal than anyone I've ever known before. He did this all because he loves us, and he walks us through all of the tragedies, trials, and tribulations we may face. He proved love always defeats fear, and it is a weapon Satan himself can never parry. In fact, love may be the most perplexing weapon against any demonic attack in history. Jesus loved his disciples, loved the people who followed him, loved the ones who didn't, and everyone else in between. This Last Supper could have been about the devil being in the room, what happened to Judas Iscariot, or even his disciples' lack of faith in Jesus' power over death. It wasn't about any of these things because Jesus trusted God implicitly, and that trust gave him the freedom to focus on loving those around him.

If Jesus could trust his Heavenly Father in that moment and be guided by his love for everyone in the room, what about you? The Last Supper of Jesus takes us down this beautiful path of giving everything in our lives over to God and showing us exactly how to love others instead of fearing what may happen. Jesus was fully committed to God's plans. Satan, however, was back on the move. The deal had been made, the plan was in motion, and the devil was still on the prowl.

Chapter 8

Pat

"I will tell you what a tragedy is. I will show you how to

waste your life. Consider a story from the February 1998

edition of Reader's Digest, which tells about a couple who

"took early retirement from their jobs in the Northeast five

years ago when he was 59 and she was 51. Now they live in

Punta Gorda, Florida, where they cruise on their 30 foot

trawler, play softball and collect shells."

Picture them before Christ at the great day of judgment:

Look, Lord. See my shells.' That is a tragedy. And people

today are spending billions of dollars to persuade you to

embrace that tragic dream. Over against that, I put my

protest: Don't buy it. Don't waste your life."

– John Piper, Don't Waste Your Life

The scent of salt air worked like a flashback inducer, launching me back into memories from two decades earlier of my summer in Virginia Beach. Nostalgia, though, eventually gave way to reality, and I came back to the summer of 2014, twenty-two years after my life-changing journey to Virginia Beach. Once more a new adventure had taken me across the country. This time was quite different as I was simply searching for some well-earned rest and relief. Ocean City, New Jersey was a random choice, but it couldn't have been better. When I wanted to get lost in the crowd around me, the local coffee shop, a diner, or the boardwalk had plenty of folks around. It was the quiet view of the Atlantic Ocean, however, especially at sunrise, that I desired most. I held captive every morning run and each unforgettable mile I ran along the boardwalk, racing against seagulls and people on those funny bikes with baskets that you only see in beach towns.

Waves crashed behind me as I sat on a wooden bench aside the moonlit boardwalk. It was the final night before my much too brief respite was over. A muscular twenty-something year old guy in a tight, pink shirt and wearing an oversized neck brace rode an old bike down the pier, barely controlling his chosen mode of transportation. I thought that it must be a joke, but then maybe he just couldn't control the bike and he really did have a neck injury. Regardless, he's dangerous. Then two different sets of parents, just moments apart, were in hot pursuit of their toddlers at top speed on their classic escape route to nowhere. It's the same route we all ran when we were little kids. There was this man in front of me and he started hacking up a lung while his wife, eating the largest soft pretzel in North America, looked away in more than obvious disdain. He did virtually nothing to conceal his blaring cough. People kept strolling in and out of my sight as night grew later. The stores started to close up for the night. The crowds had been a little crazy, and the shop employees counted down the seconds until they could pull shut their gates and lock their doors.

Humanity ebbed in and out of the crowded boardwalk while I sat there patiently taking it all in. Cru has a summer project here, and it wasn't long before their familiar approach caught my eye. About fifty feet down from me, a group of college students congregated around a couple of guys their age. The two young men were listening and sharing. They had a survey with them to draw out the dialogue if needed, but it wasn't by the look of it. They were every bit as direct as I was twenty-two years ago. I remembered it as if it were just yesterday when I was there, an idealistic college student on a beach at night sharing the goodness of God to anybody with a pulse and a second to listen to my story. I prayed for these younger and much cooler looking versions of myself while listening in from the wooden bench, indulging in the memories of a time not so long ago.

Something else, however, caught my eye just a little further down the boardwalk. Remnants of the past flooded my mind as my attention was now fixed on the street preacher and the small crowd around him. The ocean was a good bit louder than he was, but I could just pick up a little of what he was saying. All of those crazy street preacher stereotypes filled my mind, from the bad suits to the screaming about judgment and Hell. This street preacher wasn't loud, though, and he seemed to smile a lot. His crowd was interested at first, but became more and more distracted by the sights around them, until the last of them finally walked away. My entertainment here was over, and it was time to move on and head up the boardwalk for a little more adventure.

I got up and began to stroll casually in quiet reflection, continuing to take in the scene around me. My steps brought me within earshot of the street preacher, but it looked like he was done for the evening. He was packing up his easel and it hit me there might not be another opportunity to talk to him, and it was the weirdest thing, but I needed to figure something out. I don't know why I felt this massive urge to talk to him, but maybe I just had to know what made this guy tick. Before I could change my mind, I walked casually up to him and went for the home run in my first swing.

"Hi there. I'm Thad. I was wondering, why do you do this?" I said as he swiftly turned his head to see me standing there alone in front of him.

I had never spoken personally with a street preacher in depth, but I had felt drawn to this man. The idea of "street preachers" made me a little skittish, but there was something different about him. I've only had a few encounters with them over the years, but most of them had been preaching fire and brimstone, or others filled with hate, anger, and legalism, and some had a little of both. Some seemed determined to polarize the crowd around them. Brother Jerry at Wright State University was possibly the worst, calling women who walked by vile names and spewing words of damnation upon anyone he could. Occasionally he was mocked by a crowd, but he seemed well prepared for any confrontation. I was prepared for Brother Jerry, but I wasn't prepared for Pat.

He was thin and maybe an inch or two shorter than me, with piercing blue eyes. His hair was still hanging in there, but a little bit of balding appeared as his comb-over blew gently in the ocean air. His black shoes looked comfortable for walking or standing and were maybe the only things he wore that hadn't been second hand or were more than twenty years old.

"Wow. That's a really good question," he said, while dropping his head just a bit. I could tell the street preacher was trying to get a read on me, but I wasn't going to budge right now. I didn't want to mince words or have him attempt to connect with me theologically. If he was anything like the hate-spewing Brother Jerry, this conversation needed to happen without any detours.

Slowly and thoughtfully, he continued, "I guess it's just what God wants me to do. He loves these people. I'm here to talk about Him and salvation."

My eyebrows rose as the tension between us dropped flat. He didn't seem like he was some angry guy screaming about hell, but he was coming across to me as a genuine and humble man. I was quickly encouraged. His tone and gestures told the story of his humility and wide-eyed wonder of God. One thing was sure; he looked at me cautiously and appeared as interested in figuring me out as I was him.

I responded, "It's just so cool you're talking about Jesus out here on the boardwalk. What an amazing story to tell."

"Yes. Yes! He sent me here to talk about Him. He's done so much for me it just made sense."

"How long have you been coming out here?" I asked.

"Wow, I guess it's been about eight years since God brought me to the boardwalk. It just kind of started one day and never really ended."

"Sure," I said with a smile as I responded. "And this place made sense because of the number of different people you see. You know, there are some students from Cru out here who are on a summer project. Have you had much interaction with them?"

"Yes. Not all the time, but we've talked some. I like them. I'm not sure how they feel about me, but they are nice. They like doing the surveys and leading into it more slowly and I guess I've heard I move very quickly to the main points." A sweet smile touched the corner of his lips.

I had a lot more questions, but I didn't want the man to think I was speaking with him just to quiz him. I hadn't shared why I needed to talk with him, but it was time to get to the heart of it all. I asked the man, "So, do you believe it's all because of God you are able to do this?"

"Are you a Calvinist?" was the street preacher's response.

"I guess I just try to follow Jesus the best I can."

He smiled and responded slowly, "That's good. Yes. Following Jesus. It's truly why I'm out here. To talk about Jesus. You know, those folks from Cru had a preacher in at the big Baptist church here and he was amazing. He said it's not about a survey or whatever, but it's truly about saying what God leads you to say. He said it's not even about your words, as much as God giving you the words to speak. He was just phenomenal. I loved him and these students are really great!"

"What is your name? I'm so glad to have met you," I said with a big smile while extending my hand.

The older man grinned, and appearing very relieved, said, "I'm Pat."

Pat had a few questions for me, so we spent the next few moments discussing my brief sabbatical. I spoke of God's grace through some pretty hard times, and how God brought me peace. I told him how I basically jumped in the car on this adventure and maybe God brought me here just to meet Pat. I shared that I didn't have a plan, but was I was becoming more convinced by the second that God did.

Pat paused thoughtfully and said, "I started having major problems when I began coming out here, and they've continued. Everything was always fine before. I honestly feel like Job with the trials I've been hit with, and everything has been getting worse. I do feel like it's the devil trying to hurt me."

Pat spent the next few moments sharing the personal trials and attacks he had faced and continued to face. He spoke of the strained relationships and tragedies in his life since he responded to God's calling to come preach on the boardwalk. Pat took a chance and walked out here alone on that first night and has never looked back. He passionately shared his desire for everyone to understand God's love and grace, especially the ones who the Lord kept bringing into his path. Pat was sincere and hopeful, but also reserved. He knew he was in a deep spiritual battle because of the choices he had made to live a life like this.

I listened for awhile, then finally I gently said, "A friend from high school sent me an encouraging message one day. She told me, "The enemy wants nothing more than to shut you up and rob you of your joy." She wanted me to know the joy I have in God is my greatest testimony of his love."

Pat looked me dead in the eye and in a serious tone said, "Nothing like these horrible things that have been happening ever happened to me before. I came out here to preach about Jesus, and when I did, my life was thrown into absolute chaos. It really is chaos. I finally retired from teaching at the school. Most of my friends retired and bought houses in Florida and these boats, but I just couldn't bring myself to do it. It's been eight years now and I come out here because it's what God wants me to do with my time."

It grew silent for a moment. Then I looked at Pat and said, "Pat, you're leading me and others in what it looks like to love God and love people. There's this book, *Don't Waste Your Life* by a guy named John Piper. He describes a man, a man the exact opposite of you, Pat. A man who is running to Jesus at the end of his life was shouting, 'I've wasted my life! I've wasted my life.' John Piper tells inspiring stories about other men and women who didn't waste their lives, people like you, my friend. I don't know how tough it must be for you sometimes, but it's completely encouraging to me and more people than you'll probably ever know."

Pat dipped his head humbly and looked to the ground. He paused soberly, then tilted his head up and said to me, "This just seems like the best way to tell people about Jesus. I see them, you know? I see how they are searching or hurting or feel like there is no hope, but there is so much hope. I live here and there's the boardwalk, so I can see the most people here. It just made sense."

Pat and I spent some more time talking and exchanged information. I told him I didn't know when I would be back, but I'd like for him to review some of the things I'm writing, if he didn't mind. I shook his hand and walked away, leaving behind me the man whose story I would always remember. Maybe one day I will follow Pat out there. I never thought of myself as a street preacher before, but I'm sure Pat never thought he'd spend his first eight years of retirement out on the boardwalk at night in Ocean City, New Jersey, telling everyone who would listen about Jesus.

Most churches can't get a pastor to stay for four years, let alone eight. While so many ministries are bogged down in administrative functions and over-bloated processes, for more than eight years my new friend, Pat, had been carrying his easel by himself out onto the boardwalk to share God's love to the few who might give him the slightest acknowledgment of his existence. He is determined to get to the boardwalk despite the hardships he has experienced and Satan's attempts to prevent him from doing God's work.

Let's go back to Matthew 4 where Jesus stood toe-to-toe with the devil in the desert. At the pinnacle of his hunger and exhaustion, the devil arrived to tempt Jesus. Satan blitzed, understanding this was the moment when Jesus would be the most susceptible to temptation.

At any point, Jesus could have given into the devil and sinned, and no one but the Father would have known. The simplicity of the first temptation at first glance wouldn't appear to be sinful, just turning stones into bread so Jesus could have something to eat. Jesus, however, knew the devil wanted him to use his power for personal gain, and as hungry as Jesus was, he was not about to concede to Satan. What Jesus did, however, surprised the devil.

Satan commanded, "'If you are the Son of God, command these stones to become loaves of bread.' But he answered, 'It is written, "Man shall not live by bread alone, but by every word that comes from the mouth of God"'" (Matthew 4:3-4).

Jesus responded by quoting scripture, establishing his foundation in the word of God. Having a foundation in God's word is extremely crucial when you are under spiritual attack, because the truths of God's word will help you to resist the temptations of the devil. We learn from Jesus here that having knowledge of the Bible can provide specific instruction and protection when we are attacked. Jesus slammed this back to Satan and, with confidence, dismantled his first scheme against Jesus.

The devil then lead Jesus into Jerusalem, to the highest point of the city, and attempted to sway Jesus by using the scriptures against him.

Satan said, "If you are the Son of God, jump off! For the scriptures say, 'He will order his angels to protect you. And they will hold you up with their hands so you won't even hurt your foot on a stone'" (Matthew 4:6 NLT).

The devil was talking about a private demonstration of power. What could be so wrong with that? Satan understood the power of Jesus, at least more than anyone else at the time would. Jesus knew exactly who he was and what he was capable of. No one was watching, and in that moment, Jesus could show Satan exactly what kind of power he was railing against. Maybe it was time to send the devil a message.

Yet Jesus knew there was no benefit to anyone in what the devil had asked of him. Jesus had nothing to prove, yet Satan was still determined to control Jesus by attempting to exploit Jesus' identity as the Messiah. In this unforgettable moment in history, we begin to see the depths the devil would go to when attacking Jesus, and thus, what he could do when attacking us. He took what Jesus depended on and treasured most, his connection to his Father through the scriptures, and he distorted them to serve his personal purposes. Jesus understood what was happening and responded immediately, saying, "The Scriptures also say, 'You must not test the Lord your God'" (Matthew 4:7 NLT).

What was Satan's original offense in the Garden of Eden? The devil sinned by attempting to rival God himself for power. He approached Eve first with the temptation of knowledge, thus encouraging her to achieve power. He told her she'd be like God if she ate of the fruit. This spiritual attack on Jesus was the same attack Satan has been using for millenniums. He was attempting to find any potential pride in Jesus' heart and use it against him. The problem for the devil, however, was that Jesus wasn't prideful, but rather a humble and gentle Savior. No matter how hard he tried, the devil could not get Jesus to sin.

Satan tried one final attack to tempt Jesus with the things of this world and offered Jesus everything his eye could see. All he had to do was kneel before Satan and he would get everything he could possibly want in this life. Remember, Jesus was hungry and tired. He needed food and shelter and rest, and he'd been given the opportunity for that and so much more. Jesus, however, was determined. He had built a solid trust in His Father and could specifically fend off the attack in that moment by again relying on the power of his Father, his knowledge of the scriptures, and his own power, a power we will soon see knows no bounds.

From the top of a very high mountain, the devil said to Jesus, "'All these I will give you, if you will fall down and worship me.' Then Jesus said to him, 'Be gone, Satan! For it is written, "You shall worship the Lord your God and him only shall you serve"'" (Matthew 4:9-10).

The devil fled after his complete and utter failure, as Jesus had resisted temptation in his first recorded encounter with Satan. Angels came and took care of him because this wasn't some simple moment of him just saying no to the devil's offers. Jesus had just stood directly in opposition to Satan, and if he wasn't already weakened and exhausted, both physically and spiritually, from forty days of fasting and being alone in the desert, he most certainly was now. God the Father was providing for Jesus' needs after that satanic hardship as he was about to begin his final preparations to go out into the world to do things no one before or after him would ever be able to do.

Jesus and men like Pat have a deep and loyal love for the Father, and because of this love, they are joyful in their obedience to their Heavenly Father and their purpose. As we read the words of Jesus and listen to men like Pat, we discover a connection deeper than just mere ideals. We begin to understand this begins with the sacrificial love from the Father, and it becomes something we can also reflect to the world around us.

You know, I saw him again, just two years later. It was the summer of 2016, and this time I brought my wife and most of our kids back to Ocean City, New Jersey for a week of fun and relaxation on one of the best boardwalks in America. While all of us were thrilled to embark on our summer vacation, I was wondering if I'd find Pat out there. I mean, it had been two years and it's not like Pat is a young man. He'd faced hardships and so much more than I'm sure he was willing to share with me in our one fateful conversation. Instead of wandering that boardwalk alone like I did two years earlier, the seven of us stuck together while buying up New Jersey's best gelato and grey hoodies that read "Ocean City" on the front. And in the middle of the giant pizzas, bags of Brown's donuts, and crazy toddlers making their break for freedom, there he stood with two young guys listening, my old friend, Pat, and his easel, doing what he's been doing for over a decade now. I have to tell you it was one of the highlights of my trip, seeing this older man continuing to walk down the path that Jesus set for him. I was surprised he remembered me and our conversation, but maybe I shouldn't have been. Maybe I should have known our time together wasn't just for me.

Jesus defeated Satan in the desert just as Pat defeats him every single day he takes the long walk out on the Boardwalk in Ocean City. It's the same thing that happens when we pray for our friends, open our Bibles, and tell somebody how much God loves them. Nothing boils the blood of the devil like devotion and love for the Father, especially when it comes from men and women like my friend, Pat, who serve in spite of and during the trials and hardships in their life. It isn't exclusive to certain kinds of people, though. In fact, it's actually Jesus who is the author of all good stories of love and devotion. Those stories and the hope of this world are about to collide with an angry mob on its way to meet Jesus in the heart of the garden. A night filled with a great betrayal, crushing fear, and unmatched violence is about to begin. Hope, however, rises as Jesus comes up from his knees, lifts his head, and steps forward to face a darkness the world had never seen.

Chapter 9

Scaremare

"God uses broken things. It takes broken soil to produce a crop, broken clouds to give rain,

broken grain to give bread, broken bread to give strength. It is the broken alabaster box that

gives forth perfume. It is Peter, weeping bitterly, who returns to greater power than ever."

- Vance Havner

"We are so glad you're here. We've been praying for you, Thad!"

A few hours before those words were spoken I had decided this day was trash and nothing good was going to come of it. I was a twenty-three year old college student at Liberty University, and even though my world revolved pretty much around me, I was quite annoyed with my life. Probably not a huge shock, huh? My grades stunk this quarter, and I didn't have a girlfriend or the remotest possibility of one. It's a little embarrassing to admit today, but I was just way too wrapped up in my own shortcomings. This pity party was invite only and exclusive to me. On this cool, fall day, I left my dorm room, got in my car, and drove away.

My foot hit the accelerator of my light blue 1990 Ford Taurus as I entered the mountains around Lynchburg, Virginia. What I needed was time alone, but also some time to pray. Those lonely mountains were the perfect place to get my head under control, and to whine to God about what I thought I was entitled to. In my mind, this was exactly what I needed in this day of bemoaning and drudgery. Those peaceful, rolling hills in late October would surely bring me the peace I so desperately convinced myself I needed.

My roommate, Eddie Cole, had wanted me to go to Scaremare that evening with him, but I wasn't interested. Scaremare was basically a giant haunted house with the main focus being to show anyone who walked through what it would it look like if they died and didn't have a relationship with Jesus. In some circles of Christianity, these are controversial, but I thought it was pretty neat. No matter what your thoughts are on these types of events, Scaremare was a way to share the truth about God's love and the story of salvation through Jesus. Buses came from hours away to experience one of the best haunted houses and Christian events in the area.

Liberty University students worked in different capacities at Scaremare. Some worked inside the haunted house terrifying those who dared walk those frightening corridors. Other students would assemble at tents just outside the back door. As groups came out of the haunted house, they would be welcomed into the tents for some hot cocoa and to hear someone share their story about God's love and a personal testimony of what Jesus had done for them. I had been the speaker in the tent once before, and although I enjoyed several aspects of it, tonight just wasn't the night for me to be there.

Eddie had come to know Jesus only a few years earlier and had an encouraging personal story for anyone coming to God later in life. He was also a highly skilled teacher, oozing with energy and passion as he shared

God's message of hope. My friend was a perfect fit for Scaremare. His friends, other young men and women at Liberty pursuing their ministerial degrees, were leveraging their experience and talents to speak with the groups coming in and out of their tents. They were all enthusiastic and experienced. Tonight, I was miring in the depths of my own self loathing. Scaremare wasn't anywhere on my radar.

As I journeyed deeper into the mountains, I began to relax and enjoy the Fall colors. The beauty pulled me in and I began to pray while Audio Adrenaline's worship song "My Worldview" was on repeat in the background. As I tried to listen to God's leading, a deep conviction came over me and I knew I needed to repent and ask God to help pull me out of my newly acquired rotten, selfish, thankless, and stinking attitude. I was humbled and a bit embarrassed by my whining, but before I knew what was happening, a renewed energy and spirit came over me. I clung to God's forgiveness and let go of my shame. I realized the best thing for me was to get with some friends and get involved in others' lives. Even though I had only been out there for about an hour, I knew it was time to head back to campus and get with my friends.

The winding, mountain roads around Liberty were not always so easy to navigate. I realized quickly I was completely and utterly lost. Maybe I'd find the city of Roanoke up ahead, because it felt like I was heading that direction. With no clue how to get back to school from where I was, I just kept driving. And driving. If I could find a highway, I would be okay (yep, still no Google Maps). I drove aimlessly and just kept guessing, turning left and right and every which way I could think that would lead me back to Lynchburg. I had been lost in those mountains before, earlier that fall. I travelled completely in the wrong direction until I ended up not far from the border of North Carolina, which was about an hour away from Lynchburg. This time I didn't have a ton of hope I'd be back at school anytime soon. I could only hope to find a highway around Roanoke and make my way back to campus.

Finally, signs of civilization emerged as I came down a pretty steep hill into some random neighborhood of older homes. The landscape quickly changed into an industrial area, and suddenly it all looked familiar. I wasn't in Roanoke or anywhere near it. Something caught my eye on my left. I glanced over and quickly slammed on my brakes. Literally. Bewildered, I sat there completely frozen, gawking out my window.

"Ok, God. You brought me here. What do I do now?"

Breathe. Just breathe, Thad. You are here and it's for a purpose. Whatever happened before you got here doesn't matter anymore. Just be here.

My fingers clumsily dried my eyes while my spirit praised God for his goodness and his forgiveness. Pausing for just a moment to take all of this in, I finally turned left and parked my car in the small, dirt parking lot behind the massive structure. I sat there for another few seconds, completely overwhelmed. I don't know how it could have possibly happened, as I would have sworn I was off in the exact opposite direction, but somehow I was here. I finally unbuckled from the blue cloth seat inside that old Ford Taurus and half stumbled out of my car. I stood there for a moment looking at the building and then headed straight ahead. And into Scaremare.

I was at least thirty minutes late and hadn't signed up to be one of the speakers. Maybe I could just help out somehow? I could clean up trash around the tents or whatever they needed. I was embarrassed and humbled before God for my horrible, lousy attitude, and still in complete and total shock for how I ended up here, but regardless of how I felt, I started walking towards the tents. The best way to describe my feelings might be to say I was experiencing a deeply repentant humility. God had really exposed this ugly side of me, and I wanted nothing to do with it anymore. I didn't really know what to say or who to talk to when suddenly, everything got very…well…weird.

"We are so glad you're here. We've been praying for you, Thad!" said one of the two young women who ran over to greet me.

"Right," I mumbled not having any clue who they were.

"Thad! It's so good to see you again. We heard you were coming, but would be late. I think you're in Tent number one tonight," the other girl exclaimed with a smile leading me to the tent.

The first girl spoke again, "We'll be here as part of your prayer team as you speak. I think the first group is about to come to you at any minute."

My head was just spinning. First of all, I have always had a pretty solid memory of the people I've met, and the fact that two, cute college girls that I had never seen before were happy to see me had me pretty freaked out. Who were they? Liberty was a pretty big school, but this was insane. They seemed to be very familiar with me, yet I had no clue who they were. Second, I didn't tell anyone I was coming. I specifically told Eddie I wouldn't be there, and that was the only conversation I had with anyone about Scaremare. Despite all of this, not only did I have a tent, but I was assigned the first tent and would see a ton of people that night. Third, how in the world did I end up here in my car? No matter how many times I turned this over in my mind, I wasn't going to figure it out. But maybe that was the whole point.

Confused and humbled, I walked slowly into the empty tent and waited. Moving to the front of the tent, I turned to face where the group of ten to twenty people were about to walk in. Those two flaps were pulled wide open, inviting the crowd into my tent. I stood alone, waiting to tell my story to anyone willing to hear it. I didn't know what I would say, and I didn't have time to really think about it. Those two girls, who still freaked me out, walked in along with a few other volunteers, and together they prayed for me. The lesson in humility continued. I didn't deserve any of their prayers. I wasn't like the other guys there sharing Jesus' love that evening. They were experienced teachers and I was, well, just me. Something, though, was happening on this cool, October evening, and God wanted me to be there as he worked.

They said, "Amen!" and moved to the back of the tent as people began filing in and sat down on white, plastic folding chairs. I opened my mouth and began to speak. I passionately dove into the plan of God for their lives, and the story of Jesus. I don't think I really considered much of what I was saying. My mouth just opened and all kinds of words kept flying out of it.

As the night went on, group after group filed in and listened to me speak. I noticed more people throughout the night coming in to pray for me and even some of the other speakers stopped in. I didn't know what I was saying, or what to say next, but I just kept passionately speaking about God's love and his amazing grace. More and more people kept indicating they wanted to know more about a relationship with Jesus. Some invited him to be their Savior in that moment. I felt like I had no control over what I was saying, but I just kept going. Hands were going up again and again, and those wonderful prayer leaders would take folks out to share the Gospel more in depth.

My internal feelings of unworthiness and humility continued as I spoke. I barely took a break, just occasionally to warm my hands and lips with a cup of hot cocoa I was offered. People kept filing in and listening. Any idea of a planned message was gone as this shell of a guy just stood there speaking with fire and passion of the love of his Savior. A few of my friends stuck their head in and later told me it was very different hearing me speak that night. Along with the prayer leaders, my friends kept talking about how they felt different whenever they stopped in tent number one and how even the air seemed to feel different inside. I didn't know how to respond to them, so I didn't. They prayed and I spoke. Clueless as to what would come out of my mouth next, I just kept speaking.

When we finished for the night, I just stood there, a little confused, but filled with joy. Eddie stopped by to talk to me briefly and said he heard something was going on in my tent. He told me whatever it was, it felt like intense spiritual warfare as he walked by. I couldn't even begin to figure out what had just happened. I got in my car, again with a few tears hung up in my eyes. I sat there alone in the dark. One hundred thirty-nine. As I had walked away, one of the girls told me that tent number one had seen a hundred thirty-nine people making a decision to ask God to change them and to make Jesus the Lord of their life. One hundred thirty-nine. I didn't have any idea what to do with that number, or anything else that had happened to me that night. Nothing had been my doing, and no one could ever explain it except through this one phrase – "God is for you, Thad."

I never again saw either of those two girls who greeted me and told me they were praying for me at Scaremare. I asked a few of my friends, including Eddie, if they knew who I was talking about, and no one else did. In 1994, Liberty wasn't the big school that it is today, and I think somebody should have been able to tell me something. Whoever they were, they greeted me with God's love and his amazing grace. It was exactly what a humbled college guy needed and was a gift from God.

Prayer changed everything that night and left me with the deep memory and knowledge of God's love. The prayers for the broken man that I was were a colossal part of my night at Scaremare. Prayer has always been one of the most important blessings in my life. The idea of the freedom and power we have to communicate directly with the God of the Universe is borderline ridiculous, and our access to him is unparalleled. I couldn't believe he wanted anything to do with the likes of me, and it was unbelievable what God chose to do through me that night. While others were praying for me in confidence of what God would do, I was coming to him on my knees begging for a clue.

Two thousand years earlier, with his friends nearby, Jesus begins to process a future no one else would be able to imagine. As he walked down a road that no one could go down with him, he knew the Father was close and would not leave him. Jesus was now face-to-face with his destiny. The time had come to fulfill his purpose for coming to the world, the home of murderers, rapists, thieves, liars, porn addicts, abusers, self-seeking narcissists, and drunks. He wasn't here for only the best of us, and he didn't come just to save the worst. Jesus had come to be the sacrificial lamb for everyone, no matter who they are and no matter what they've done.

The final moments of whatever calm Jesus might have had in his life were about to end as he stepped into the Garden of Gethsemane. He had prepared his heart and mind and was ready to stand before a force of men beyond what any one man alone could have ever endured. He had always known what lay before him.

Jesus and his disciples were entrenched in the building tension that swirled around them, especially since Jesus' actions at the temple after his arrival on Palm Sunday in Jerusalem. The Pharisees and elders of the people would not stand for anymore of what Jesus had been preaching, and the story of Lazarus had made his presence in their city intolerable. To find a moment of peace, Jesus took Peter, James, and John and headed into the Garden of Gethsemane.

"And he said to his disciples, 'Sit here, while I go over there and pray'" (Matthew 26:36).

The once precarious mood had now changed as Jesus looked to them and said, "My soul is very sorrowful, even to death; remain here, and watch with me" (Matthew 26:38).

He walked deeper into the garden, away from his disciples, seeking solitude and prayer. Jesus began to pray, but quickly returned to find his friends sleeping. He left them again, but soon came back to find them asleep once more. Leaving them one final time, Jesus stepped away to spend time with his Father in an iconic time of prayer.

> Father, the hour has come; glorify your Son that the Son may glorify you, since you have given

him authority over all flesh, to give eternal life to all whom you have given him. And this is eternal life, that they know you, the only true God, and Jesus Christ whom you have sent. I glorified you on earth, having accomplished the work that you gave me to do. And now, Father, glorify me in your own presence with the glory that I had with you before the world existed. I have manifested your name to the people whom you gave me out of the world. Yours they were, and you gave them to me, and they have kept your word. Now they know that everything that you have given me is from you. For I have given them the words that you gave me, and they have received them and have come to know in truth that I came from you; and they have believed that you sent me. I am praying for them. I am not praying for the world but for those whom you have given me, for they are yours. All mine are yours, and yours are mine, and I am glorified in them." (John 17:1-10).

What the disciples didn't know was that an army was on the brink of coming through the garden and capturing Jesus. In that moment, however, something else was on Jesus' mind. His disciples were about to flee for their lives, yet Jesus' prayer was not filled with remorse or fear, but rather with praise for his Father. It was also emphatically filled with hope for man. Jesus had nothing short of great expectations, and he passionately implored the Father to protect and show his love to every one of his followers. He was praying for God's glory to remain in him, and for Christians to reflect the goodness, love, and glory of God. He was not only asking God for help, but identifying his followers as being deeply connected to him and to God himself. It was a specific and focused prayer for all the followers of Jesus, coming from Jesus to God the Father just as Jesus was about to be seized and brought to trial. Jesus was not waiting silently. He was pursuing God's will actively through deeply devout prayer and unwavering hope.

Throughout this incredible chapter of John 17, which is also known as the High Priestly Prayer, Jesus claimed an identity of him being with the Father and for us being identified in Jesus. This was the purpose and journey of Jesus Christ, and exactly why he came to earth. We needed a Savior. We needed the Son of God to come and fight against evil once and for all and to create a way for us to have a true relationship with God. Jesus knew all of this, and his prayer here is for you to join him in the glory and marvel of knowing God. If there is ever an identity you need most, it is the one you have waiting for you in Jesus.

There is a level of discomfort that arises in me as Jesus spoke of this ultimate reflection of himself reflecting God, and for our lives to also glorify God and the life he lived. I sometimes wonder why God chooses people who are as frail and weak as me to reflect his glory. If we truly delve deep into the truth that lies within our hearts, I don't know how anyone on their own can reconcile this. How does a sinful man in this world today consistently reflect God and glorify Jesus with his life? This is like putting together a team of NBA All-Stars and asking me to come be their starting Center. First of all, I'm about eight inches too short, and secondly, I stink at basketball. I could say I'd give my best effort, but that effort would look ridiculous next to someone like Lebron James or Michael Jordan in his prime. Actually, it would be ridiculous when neither of them are in their prime. I would have some potential, as almost anyone would, to find a way to dunk a basketball or make a good play on the court. Given enough training and opportunity, almost anyone in their prime could play basketball, even at a high level. What are the chances, however, that I would be able to, let's say, part the Red Sea? If I worked super hard and brought a huge focus, would I possibly ever be able to raise my friend from the dead or send an angel to slaughter an opposing army for me? Could I conceive creating another world, and then actually do it? Well, since I can barely conceive cooking a meal from scratch, I think I know my limitations.

Unworthiness is the first word that strikes me when I consider Jesus' prayer of being glorified through us. I think the second word that comes to me is humbled. Was Jesus glorified when my temper got the best of my thoughts after I was cut off on the highway? Was Jesus glorified when I used to weigh close to four hundred pounds and would drive through McDonald's ordering (follow me here) two of the 2 for $2 Big Mac Specials and consume all four Big Macs in record time in the front seat of my magical, blue Ford Taurus? How did my life glorify Jesus when I was a jerk to my kids? Does a bad attitude at home reflect Jesus?

In many cases, we are left feeling overwhelmed, unworthy, and like a complete fraud, and too often this is where our story ends. We creep into guilt and self-loathing, and finally, hopefully, there is a slow and monotonous repentance. It is not, however, the way God intends for us to be. God is not looking for us to walk around with our heads down muttering words of unworthiness and harboring deep feelings of guilt for our inadequacies. As intense as the High Priestly Prayer here is, Jesus demonstrates the special place we hold in the heart of God and how God is constantly working in our lives. God has purposed us to glorify his name and to believe he will help us know how to glorify him.

There is only one word which can help us reconcile any of this properly, and that word is love. God must have an amazing love for you to allow you to be part of something so ridiculously blessed as a relationship with him as described in John 17. The colossal love of God is a love so amazing and so all encompassing, we frankly don't really know what to do with it.

Jesus is bringing all of our weird, weak, and sinful selves into a complete identity in him. He is not afraid for us to be identified in him, and God glorifies anyone who is with Jesus. God is not concerned about what you will do to his reputation, and Jesus never carried around a fragile ego, trying to protect his image, especially when times got tough. He is saying quite deliberately in this scripture that we are united and bonded to him, and that our identities are completely connected.

It honestly makes me feel like the prodigal son, or some vagabond outcast who is continuously outgunned when trying to live up to the righteous standard set by Christ. Jesus, however, isn't sitting in a corner, checking off our legalistic activities and numbering how many good deeds we've performed. He is looking at our hearts and looking for us to embrace the love he offers each of us. It's ok to feel like the prodigal son or an unworthy Christian, because if we didn't, I don't think we would truly grasp the level of love and grace God has shown us.

Some of you are reading this and thinking you might be disqualified from God's love. It's ok if you feel this way, because I sometimes feel this way, too. It doesn't matter, though, how you feel, because feelings are not always aligned with the truth. Jesus is ready for all adulterers, hypocrites, porn addicts, workaholics, alcoholics, drug abusers, cheaters, murderers, rapists, liars, and everyone else in between to be identified with him. If you are willing to embrace the love of Jesus and follow him for the rest of your life, your identity is now found in him. It is you he was praying for in the Garden that night. It is you he has hope for and loves just as you are right now.

Chapter 10

Mob

Pippin: There's no more stars. Is it time?

Gandalf: Yes.

Pippin: It's so quiet...

Gandalf: It's the deep breath before the plunge.

Pippin: I don't want to be in a battle. But waiting on the edge of one I can't escape is even worse. Is there any hope, Gandalf?

- The Lord of the Rings: The Return of the King (2003)

It was a perfect island morning on February 22nd, 2015, and Melanie and I started day two of our honeymoon off early, both of us up and moving before 7AM. We lazily opened the front door and slowly walked about fifty feet down to the beach, each toting a glorious mug of Honduran coffee. Step by step, we took the long walk out onto the dock, climbing the stairs to the top deck out on the long dock. There we met Pete, Catherine, William, Phyllis, and we saw our favorite missionaries, Bob and Debi. We dropped gently into the deck chairs as the morning breeze and warm air off of the ocean filled us with hope and the thrill of a new day of adventures.

For our honeymoon, we had flown to the Island of Roatan, Honduras, for a time of rest, celebration, and all kinds of fun. From zip lines to snorkeling to radiant sunsets stretching for a thousand miles over the calm ocean waters, everything, and yet nothing, was going as planned. When we arrived, we met some of the nicest folks you'd ever meet, all staying at the Sea Dancer with us. One couple, Bob and Debi Cowan, invited us to their apartment for dinner in what turned out to be a conversation of eternal proportions.

"Hey honeymooners! Honeymooners!" a shout came from outside of our front balcony.

Opening the door, I looked down to see Debi leaning over her railing from her balcony below and looking up at me with a big grin.

"I cooked way too much food...again. Do you want to come down for some homemade tacos?"

Impulsively blowing off our dinner plans, I jumped on the opportunity for free food and, without consulting my far-better-half, shouted back, "Sure thing! We'll be down in a few."

The tacos were perfect, and Melanie was quickly adjusting our grocery list to include tacos. My wife is beyond the best cook, and when we do the "Thankful for you!" game, almost everyone attests that she is the BOMB in the kitchen.

"You're missionaries? Here?" I muttered in exclamation with my cheeks packed full of Debi's tacos, as my beautiful bride looked on in horror.

With my attention fixated solely on those delicious tacos, you might not be surprised to know it took me forever and a day to deduce that Bob and Debi were missionaries to the native Hondurans on the island. What a marvelous thrill to show up in a different country and be immediately greeted by a couple who have dedicated their lives to proclaiming the story of Jesus in a foreign land! Later in this book, we'll dive a little more into the story of our missionary friends on the Island of Roatan, but for now there's someone else's story to tell.

The tacos from the night before had digested nicely and, after a peaceful morning on the dock, we decided to take Bob and Debi up on their invitation to join them for church that day. We hustled inside around 9:00am to made a couple of shakes and put on our best clothes possible for church. Melanie went with a pair of capri's and short sleeve shirt, but right before we left, Debi showed up in a sundress and let her know it was cool to wear something more casual to church. Melanie embraced the idea, flew in and changed into the original outfit she wanted to wear, and we were soon off on another adventure.

The church culture on Roatan is quite a bit different than what we might encounter in our country. Some of the churches are extremely old school where women will wear long skirts and long sleeve shirts regardless of how hot it is outside and how little air conditioning is in the church itself. It's a culture fighting the old Western virtues of conservatism that were established over sixty years ago when Honduras was gifted Roatan back by the British. Many of the Spaniards from the mainland clung to a more legalistic bent, but the native Roatans weren't so much. We walked into a church whose congregants are mostly native to the island and, from what I later learned, is also a mixture of very rich and very poor, with not so much in-between.

The rowdy kids who were there for the children's Sunday school were bellowing out their final song as we sat down in one of the pews. There must have been at least a hundred kids surrounding us. With the boys in khakis and dress shirts and the little girls wearing picture perfect summer dresses, there wasn't a kid who wasn't smiling, and their gratefulness for being there that morning was written all over their bright and smiling faces. With a hearty, two-handed handshake and his big southern accent booming, Melanie and I were greeted by the young pastor.

"New Hampshire! Well, I haven't been there before! Born and raised and lived my whole life in South Carolina, but now this beautiful island is our home," he said enthusiastically, grinning from ear-to-ear.

Bob and Debi later shared that the pastor and his wife were sent here the previous year as missionaries from the Church of God. With most of the men in ties and the women in dresses, and all of us singing from hymn books to the piano, this place brought back a flood of memories from my childhood when I attended a traditional church. After the singing came to an end, the mood suddenly shifted, and it happened all because of one man.

One of the native black Hondurans sauntered to the front of the sanctuary, slowly knelt down, and leaned into the steps of the stage, praying. The little pastor went over and hugged the now slightly trembling man. It was a little awkward, and no one seemed to even breathe except for the pianist who had the good sense to fill the void with quiet music. We were all watching and waiting for something to happen, but the pastor continued to kneel next to the large man until he gently raised him slowly up and off of his knees. The pastor then stared directly at the congregation as he and the man, with his head hung low, turned together, arm-in-arm, to the waiting group as the music came to a sudden halt. The pastor, in his thick South Carolina accent, began to address his church.

"This here is my friend, Edwin," he said, staring into the eyes of the congregants as he lowered his tone. I clung to the humanity of this moment for a second as this little, white Southern preacher stood with his arm around a very large, black Honduran man. The pastor continued, "And he is standing here today with me and I stand with him. Now there are all kinds of nasty things being said about my friend. There are lies and gossip going all over this island about him and some of it is even happening right here in this church. And it *will* stop."

The pastor's eyes seemed to grow in size as he looked across the room at everyone in his congregation. Not a single one of us dared to move or make a sound. We all sat still and held our breaths, like little kids just before they take the big plunge off their very first diving board. Edwin seemed to stand just a little taller, if possible, yet still appeared so very hurt and humbled. The pastor, however, was full of a deep resolve on that warm Sunday morning. Apparently, part of his resolve was to use this moment of uncomfortable silence to draw out his point. After what felt like an eternity, he finally spoke again.

"We will not gossip here. This is a sin and we will have no part of it. I want to be very clear. We will have no part in this as a church. And we are praying for you and your family, Edwin. I stand with you, my brother. Together this church stands with you and we are praying for you. And I want you to know right now that God is for you, Edwin. And he is for all of us who follow Jesus."

"Turn to Romans 8:31-33 in your bibles," the pastor continued. "The scripture reads, 'What then shall we say to these things? If God is for us, who can be against us? He who did not spare his own Son but gave him up for us all, how will he not also with him graciously give us all things? Who shall bring any charge against God's elect? It is God who justifies.'"

"You see that, my friend? Do you see that? As he is for everyone here, God is for you, Edwin. God is for you, my friend."

The pastor stood in silence, still with that little arm of his draped high upon Edwin's massive shoulders. Edwin's body continued to shake a little as he fought back those dreaded tears in his eyes. The very broken man tilted his head slightly down towards the pastor and gave him an exhausted but happy nod. Slowly, the little pastor escorted Edwin back to sit with his family near the front of the church. Then he turned and quickly stepped back up to the front, prayed, and began to teach. He was very passionate, but more than anything, he continued to repeat again and again how much God loves us and how important it is for each of us to understand that God is for us.

Melanie and I both choked back tears at different points throughout the service, and we knew we were experiencing God in a very exciting way. As the service ended, I bolted quickly across the church to find Edwin. Looking at him I saw a man with a story so similar to my own, but his pastor had done something beautiful, something no one had ever done for me. To say I was inspired by this moment would be a massive understatement. Edwin and I talked privately for a few minutes and he struck me as a very warm and gentle man who was enduring the horrible lies and rumors being spread about him. They were the kind of things that bring a large man to his knees in front of hundreds of his neighbors and friends. The kind of things that can break you and make you feel like no one is for you anymore. The pastor, though, made the truth very clear, and I don't think any of us dared to question it, even though we all have sometimes in the darkest places of our hearts. *God is for you.*

I never found out what happened to my new friend, Edwin, after that day, but I could relate a little to the feelings of being falsely accused of something I didn't do. I think we have all experienced this in some way, though maybe your story isn't quite as dramatic as Edwin's. I'm not sure to what degree Edwin had truly been broken, or how far down into the pits those rumors had truly dragged his weary soul, but I do know he was in the right place on February 22nd, 2015. Jesus, more than anyone, could relate to our friend, Edwin, but in his case, he already knew what was going to happen to him in the next twenty-four hours. And none of it was good.

Waiting quietly into the late hours of the night, eleven disciples remained at the Garden of Gethsemane with Jesus. The man he once called friend, Judas Iscariot, was closing in fast with an angry mob of violent soldiers and malicious religious leaders. They were getting closer and would soon come bursting onto the grounds. Jesus stepped away from the others with only Peter, James, and John. He wanted them to walk this final road with him, into the heart of the garden. If the disciples could have foreseen that night and what was about to happen, I'm quite sure some of them would have tried to grab Jesus and make a run for it. Despite the warnings from Jesus himself, they never saw any of it coming. How could they? How could they believe men would be capable of such evil?

A cold and sorrowful darkness had fallen over Jesus in his new found sadness, yet he was full of determination. His closest disciples were supposed to keep watch, but they were fast asleep. The men Judas led had been waiting for this day since Jesus resurrected Lazarus from the dead. The intensity of this pivotal moment in the garden was about to extend its reach from the world we see into the deepest chasms of hell to the heights of the heavens. We enter one of the most riveting moments in all of the scriptures as Judas, who had been a close follower of Jesus, had become indwelt by Satan and was bringing a powerful and angry mob to arrest this one man, Jesus the Christ. His disciples were still with him, but those followers of Jesus were no warriors. They were fishermen, a tax collector, and a few other assorted gentile men. Jesus was about to be badly outnumbered and outgunned. Judas seemed to have all the advantage and nothing to fear, but I think he was very afraid. Jesus was the ultimate threat to the devil, and if Satan was still indwelling Judas, he was very likely wrought with fear.

Despite the lies, rumors, and pure evil that had run amuck all around him, Jesus was the Son of God, and the devil knew the kind of power he could yield. Something seemed quite odd, though, since Jesus did not seem interested in going to battle for himself against Satan. It was almost as if Satan was allowed to do whatever he wanted to Jesus, and if that was the case, the devil was definitely going to use his powers to take Jesus' life. If Jesus actually chose to fight back, the devil and everyone with him would be destroyed. In their first encounter in the desert, however, Jesus did not destroy the devil. Whatever the devil thought he knew, we can't be certain, but he had a plan and it was all coalescing now.

God, however, saw that whole night unfolding before the creation of this world, and in his knowledge and grace, our Father allowed everything to continue. It was no surprise to him or Jesus, who had been reminding his disciples for months now of his ultimate purpose on this earth. Jesus was quite aware of the pending betrayals and the sacrifice he would have to make for all of mankind. While shouldering that burden, Jesus was also preparing his disciples for what was coming and their role in all of it. Satan was executing his plan, yet he was utterly clueless as to the true mission of Jesus and his actual role that was yet to be played.

In the heart of the garden, Jesus implored Peter, James, and John saying, "Sit here, while I go over there and pray" (Matthew 26:36).

> Then he said to them, "My soul is very sorrowful, even to death; remain here, and watch with me." And going a little farther he fell on his face and prayed, saying, "My Father, if it be possible, let this cup pass from me; nevertheless, not as I will, but as you will." And he came to the disciples and found them sleeping. And he said to Peter, "So, could you not watch with me one hour? Watch and pray that you may not enter into temptation. The spirit indeed is willing, but the flesh is weak." Again, for the second time, he went away and prayed, "My Father, if this cannot pass unless I drink it, your will be done." And again he came and found them sleeping, for their eyes were heavy. So, leaving them again, he went away and prayed for the third time, saying the same words again. (Matthew 26:38-44).

Three times he went back to them, and each time they were asleep. After everything they'd been through, and regardless of his countless warnings and the urgency in his voice, his disciples struggled to stay awake. Jesus wanted time to pray, but his time had almost run out. Judas had now entered the Garden and the disciples were powerless to help Jesus.

> While he was still speaking, Judas came, one of the twelve, and with him a great crowd with swords and clubs, from the chief priests and the elders of the people. Now the betrayer had given them a sign, saying, "The one I will kiss is the man; seize him." And he came up to Jesus at once and said, "Greetings, Rabbi!" And he kissed him. Jesus said to him, "Friend, do what you came to do." Then they came up and laid hands on Jesus and seized him (Matthew 26:47-50).

A kiss. A simple and sweet expression of love was the method used by the disciple of Jesus to put into motion the plan of Satan. It doesn't sit very well, does it, the use of a kiss to betray Jesus? Couldn't Judas have just walked up and pointed to Jesus and identified him? Wouldn't just saying his name have been enough?

Have you ever been betrayed? Were you ever deceived or mistreated by someone you cared deeply for? Did something shocking ever happen to you, leaving you confused and hurt? Jesus experienced all of this, and so much more than me, you or our friend Edwin ever experienced. In this betrayal, we see years of Jesus' work of ministering to someone he loved get tossed out the window for thirty pieces of silver, which is about $12,000 in today's wages.

Who would you betray for $12,000? Is there an innocent person you would be tempted to deceive and conspire against, knowing that it will lead to their death? If there was no chance you would be punished legally, would you willingly help plot someone's death for this amount of money? I'm sure you are as appalled as I am in considering this idea, but don't be too sure Judas was the only one willing to betray God for money. It happens all the time in our culture today, it's just often a little more cloaked and indirect.

The mob followed their leader, Judas Iscariot, into the heart of The Garden of Gethsemane and the whole world launched into chaos. Some of the disciples fled, while some stayed to fight. One of the disciples picked up a sword and moved to defend Jesus, cutting off the ear of one of the servants of the high priest.

"Put your sword back into its place. For all who take the sword will perish by the sword. Do you think that I cannot appeal to my Father, and he will at once send me more than twelve legions of angels?" (Matthew 26:52-53).

In the midst of the betrayal and the aggression from the angry mob, Jesus never lost sight of who he was and his true identity in the Father. The stress and intensity of the moment had zero affect on Jesus. He was determined to obey God and fulfill the prophecy, and nothing was going to stop it from happening. Jesus knew the power that lay within the Father, and he knew that one angel could easily take out that entire mob. It was irrelevant to Jesus whether or not he could be saved by either the Father or men. He already knew how his story was going to unfold.

"'No more of this!'" Jesus exclaimed in Luke 22:51. "And he touched his ear and healed him."

Jesus possessed a power unlike anything anyone had ever seen. Since he extended amazing grace and healed the servant's ear, couldn't we agree he could have also done something to save himself from this mob? Of course he could, but the mission of Jesus Christ was never to save himself, but to save *us*. Not only did Jesus show his remarkable power, but more than anything, he again showed remarkable humility and self-control.

Each interaction with Judas Iscariot throughout the Gospels demonstrated Jesus' self-control. Every time an enemy approached him to attempt to out him as some bad magician, Jesus consistently showed love and grace. Sometimes this love was in the form of speaking some hard truths, and the truth was incredibly important to Jesus. He didn't come to play politics or to mince words. Even in his most intense conversations, Jesus set the highest bar as he demonstrated self-control and a spectacular hope for a new beginning.

The disciples continued to run away as Jesus proceeded to speak to his accusers, saying, "Have you come out as against a robber, with swords and clubs to capture me? Day after day I was with you in the temple teaching, and you did not seize me. But let the Scriptures be fulfilled" (Mark 14:48-49).

Now Jesus stood nearly alone before the enraged and overwhelming mob. With the tiniest of efforts, he could have manipulated them and turned them into fools, but thoughts of this nature were a million miles away from the brilliant and heroic Son of God. Jesus was a straight shooter and his words and actions were for a purpose. There had to be a reason he stood by and let the mob come to take him. There must have been a purpose to all of this.

As those men stood before him in all of their anger, the Son of God chose to just be still. He was determined to fulfill the declarations of God's chosen prophets who came hundreds, and some even thousands of years earlier. Jesus tenaciously lived within his purpose, even though he knew the horrors he was about to face. I can't imagine what he felt, knowing what was coming. As he stood, as they stared at him, he knew he was going to die at their hands.

Jesus could have blamed Judas, but he would have missed the real menace here. I could have blamed others for the trials and tribulations in my life, but I also would have drastically been misled. It was the devil who was in another Garden about four thousand years earlier tempting a woman named Eve. He was the same monster who went after Job. It was the devil who sat with Jesus at the table and left to collect his silver and betray Jesus. It was the devil who also attempted to rip my life limb from limb. It was always the devil, and he is still the one behind all of the evil we see in our world today.

We have seen throughout the history of the scriptures how Satan hates us and wants nothing more than to tear down the people who love God. Actually, he wants to rip apart everyone he can, and in the Garden of Gethsemane he made his biggest move against the Savior this world desperately needs. There is something else, however, about the devil we may have missed.

When we look at Satan's approach, first in the Garden of Eden with Adam and Eve, then with Job, to his days of tempting Jesus in the desert, and finally here in Gethsemane, we see Satan was deeply troubled by God's power around him. The devil had (and still has) little power to do anything to God's people. Before he attacked Job, he had to get permission, and after he was done, God not only restored Job, but the story of Job has now brought hope to millions of people who suffer for no clear reason. As the former brightest of God's angels, Satan, for all of his power in this world, suffers defeat after defeat at the mighty hands of our Father in Heaven. In fact, Satan's plans often are just the precursor for God doing something beautiful and miraculous in our lives. What the devil means to use to destroy us, God takes and turns into something powerful and encouraging. My personal testimony, and maybe even yours, is filled with these stories. Jesus' life was about to become the greatest example in history of how the evil devices and horrific plans of Satan are captured and repurposed by God himself to create something beautiful and good.

Judas and his angry mob marched into the heart of the garden, captured Jesus and ripped him away from his friends. John ran out of there so fast he left his clothing behind. We don't know where the other disciples went, but a confused Peter was all that remained. He was left with Jesus' final words to him before the cross

"Put your sword into its sheath; shall I not drink the cup that the Father has given me?" (John 18:11).

The defensiveness of Peter was on full display when Jesus spoke of being a sacrifice for man and that his death was coming soon. Peter wanted to fight for Jesus and he made that abundantly clear throughout the Gospels. Peter was often the disciple who spoke first and then thought about it later, and I think we all have someone like that in our lives. Sometimes, actually, we *are* the ones who are just like Peter. In this powerful moment of Jesus being taken, he not only told Peter not to fight, but in Luke 18:51, Jesus healed the wounded man's ear. Peter was mad, which makes sense, but Jesus refused to be removed from the Father's will.

When I lived in the South, my friends would sometimes use the expression, "Big Hat. No Cattle." Basically, it's a southern saying which means somebody is acting like they're pretty impressive, but it might just be a big show. I think sometimes Peter fits into this category, and me, too. Peter truly loved Jesus and wanted to do his best for Jesus, but Peter was still a sinful man, and he still had plenty to learn.

My first memories include being raised in the church. Throughout my years, when I have been part of different studies on the life of Jesus, the disciple I most connected with was the highly energetic, quick to assume, first to speak, and first to put his foot in his mouth Peter. I wonder if maybe you feel this way. I wonder if Peter's life, decisions, passions, and screw-up's feel more real and familiar to you than anyone else who followed Jesus.

Do you feel as if you have been sifted? Has your life turned to chaos in a heartbeat? Have you ever been too quick to act or to say something, and then wish you hadn't put your foot in your mouth? I am totally like Peter in this respect! I told all of my friends there was no way Mitt Romney would lose the Presidency. I said that even after it was pretty certain he would lose. I am also a Cubs fan, and maybe it's enough to just say that and you can understand. Before 2016, and can I just tell you 2016 was totally the greatest year in the history of baseball, my Cubs hadn't won a World Series since 1908. Every year, though, no matter how bad the team might have been, I will tell everyone I know they are going to win it all! Go Cubbies!

Peter continued to screw up massively, but he passionately loved Jesus and continuously showed his devotion. Yes, he went on to deny Jesus three times, as Christ told him he would, but that wasn't the end of Peter's story, not by a long shot. I think many of us connect deeply with Peter because we see how Jesus loved him and kept him close, despite his incredible mistakes. I think Jesus wants us all to know he loves us just as we are. It isn't the best or the worst of us Jesus loves, he just loves us. He takes us right as we are in each moment, which is pretty humbling and not so easy to understand.

Do you have a moment in your past you truly struggle with? Is there a sin or event that once happened to you and you just can't figure out what God was doing or why it happened? If you do have a struggle like this, you should know there are a lot of us out there like you. We can never match the standard Jesus set for our lives, but this doesn't mean we don't still do our best. Peter's strength was that he kept coming back and fighting. He never fell into despair and lost faith. Maybe how I connect with Peter the most is his love for Jesus and his passion to continue growing closer to him. He wasn't perfect, but God still used him in many amazing ways.

Jesus was taken away by the mob and the disciples were scattered. After all he had done, Judas went to a field and took his own life. Darkness had set in deeply all around Jerusalem and Jesus was about to stand trial in a court which already had convicted him in their hearts. No defense would save him. God, though, still had a plan.

Jesus knew the Father loved him and had good plans for him, and like we read in Romans 8:31, that God was for him. God's plan to give Jesus to our world as our Savior was still transpiring, despite the events that just took place. Satan thought he may actually have the victory, but God wasn't finished. Jesus was about to go before the Pharisees, and even they wouldn't believe what he did next.

Chapter 11

Bullies and the Battalion

Todd Anderson: O Captain! My Captain!

Mr. Nolan: Sit down, Mr. Anderson! Do you hear me? Sit down! Sit down! This is your final warning, Anderson. How dare you? Do you hear me?

Knox Overstreet: O Captain! My Captain!

Mr. Nolan: Mr. Overstreet, I warn you! Sit down!

Mr. Nolan: Sit down! Sit down. All of you. I want you seated. Sit down. Leave, Mr. Keating. All of you, down. I want you seated. Do you hear me? Sit down!

-Dead Poets Society (1989)

As much as I hoped the boys in the iconic final scene from the movie *Dead Poets Society* were rewarded for their courage and for standing up to the bully, Mr. Nolan, my hunch is they would have eventually suffered a similar fate as their "Captain". Their "Captain", Poetry teacher John Keating played by Robin Williams, was the inspirational leader of his students. When Mr. Keating suffered a deeply emotional and undeserved ending to his career, it appeared Mr. Nolan had completed his mission and claimed the victory. In this climactic scene, however, even though Mr. Keating had just been terminated from his position and was leaving his students, his love and purpose could not be squelched. Even in the darkest moments of this story, we could see the new hope for his boys that was being born. I, however, was never strong enough to stand up to my bullies. That doesn't mean that one day my story won't also possess a courageous ending. Of course, my ending pales in comparison to the bullies Jesus was about to face.

The double glass doors had a dark tint so no one on the outside of my school could see in. My head shifted right, then left, and straight ahead as I carefully looked at my surroundings, making sure my path home was clear. From what I could see, it was safe, but these boys could close the gap on me in almost no time. Most of them were faster than me, but I was pretty strong. They never fought me one on one, but it was never one on one before anyway. They were always together in a group of at least four, although sometimes there were more.

The start of my eighth grade year was a time of transition. My parents thought it would be good for me to venture into an unchartered territory, so they decided to pull me out of the small Christian school I had been attending and move me into the public middle school. Franklin Middle School in Wheaton, Illinois seemed enormous and quite a bit confusing to the new kid who had grown up in private schools. The first few days, surprisingly, went quite well. I was the new kid and early on it seemed like everyone wanted to get to know me. I had been an awkward young man before my arrival, often trying too hard to make friends. My over-amped-up efforts were well intended, but almost always fell flat. The other eighth graders stereotyped me after a few short days, and I quickly went from being the cool, new kid to being a big time dork.

The bullying kicked into high gear when a kid named Tom hit me in the back of my head while sitting behind me in class with the giant ring on his finger. The story was that his Dad had given it him, and it seemed like he was always showing it off. One day, he kept playing with it in our health class and whispering to me that he was going to hit me with his ring. Sure enough, a few minutes later he had snuck up behind me and punched the back of my head, causing my head to launch forward and smack the desk with a loud crack. I immediately jumped up to try to defend myself, but suddenly my head burst into pain and I crumpled to the ground. The teacher sent both of us to see the principal. We left the class alone and I had to walk for a few minutes down those long halls with Tom, which is just crazy to think about today. Putting me side-by-side with my assailant wasn't probably a wise move, but Tom was really freaking out about seeing the principal, as he should have been. He kept telling me the whole way there he didn't mean to hit me with the ring and said he would leave me alone, and even be my friend, if I didn't get him in trouble. When we got there, I covered for Tom with the secretary, who listened and nodded and then sent us both back to class. Nothing actually changed for me after that with Tom, except that he seemed to ignore me a little more.

The two main groups I was dealing with now were far more difficult than just handling Tom. Brook led a group of three other boys, all smaller than me, but together they could do some damage. Then there was the group led by a kid named Rich, and he had maybe seven to eight others boys who seemed to be at his command. Rich was the fastest runner in the school, and if they were chasing me, I was toast. Rich's group was more focused on jumping me whenever they could create the opportunity, while Brook's aim was to come after me whenever he randomly spotted me. I planned my route home carefully each day, keeping careful watch for my antagonizers. At top speed, I would cut through neighbors' yards. The fences were helpful and hurtful. They were helpful in the sense that I knew where they were and how to get over or around them quickly, but they were hurtful because they could slow me down just enough so one of them could grab me. Somehow, in my three weeks at Franklin Middle School, I was able to avoid Rich's group, but eventually I went the wrong direction and came face to face with Brook and his little mob. Together they circled me like wolves hunting their prey. One of the boys rushed me from behind, got me to the ground, and held me down as the others got a few shots in. Desperate, I suddenly threw a series of wild punches, eventually connecting my fist with Brook's cheek. He went down quick. His friends were stunned and I sprinted safely home.

As difficult as Tom and the two gangs of bullies were, nothing compared to Ron. Ron was a new kind of vicious and the type of bully I hadn't ever encountered before. The very first time I spotted him in the hallway, I quickly realized the importance of avoiding him. He was volatile and had a mean streak like almost no one I'd ever encountered. He randomly slapped and shoved kids, almost as if it was a way of life for him - almost as if he enjoyed it.

Class was going to start soon, and I had to move it if I was going to make it on time. I wasn't paying attention and suddenly bumped into the person I least wanted to ever bump into. Ron. He quickly flashed a smirk at me, shoved me, and yelled some name at me as I sailed back. Catching my balance, I quickly hustled off the other direction. Ron wasn't done with me yet, though. This one moment started a chain reaction and he began to look for me each day for a quick shove and a few cruel words. Sometimes I just got shoved. Sometimes I got slapped in the face. Day after day I tried to hide from or just avoid Ron, but I couldn't keep him away. It got worse. It eventually turned a very nasty corner.

Ron started spitting on me. First he spit towards me and then just on me, and finally he started spitting in my face. I thought of fighting back, but the futile efforts I made in the past always failed. I was clumsy and slow, and even my karate lessons were useless against this man-child. I was a big kid, but he was the biggest kid in our school. Even if I could sucker punch him, I knew I would get hurt twice as bad as he would. The beatings and abuse I bore at his hands were fast and unemotional. He received just enough satisfaction hurting me, and then quickly moved on. One day he slapped one my only friend's, a kid named John, in the face. John was much smaller and weaker, but Ron still slapped him as hard as he could. John was a little bit of a different kid, and out of nowhere, and to all of our surprise, he knocked Ron back with all of his might.

Ron went flying backwards, but recovered quickly, and then punched John as hard as he could in the stomach. My friend went down, and Ron yelled, "Why can't you be like Thad? He just takes my beatings and doesn't fight back. It's always better for you if you don't fight back."

This was not my shining moment. After just three weeks at Franklin Middle School, my parents removed me and placed me back into the small Christian school I had attended previously. I never saw Ron, Brook or Rich again, even though I lived only a block and a half from Franklin. I don't remember feeling the need to avoid them anymore, and I'm sure they forgot me as quickly as

I left my beatings behind. My little school welcomed me back with open arms, and I was very happy for a some peace and a more calm educational environment for the remainder of that year.

My family moved to Ohio at the beginning of the following year, and I went to a large Christian school in the area. I was a chubby freshman and still very awkward. Though I had gained some confidence during the rest of my eighth grade year, life again turned ugly for me. The new bullies discovered me, and I was right back where I didn't ever want to be again. For most of my freshman year they antagonized me, but it soon become a way of life. Over time, I at least became a little more street smart and better at avoiding the pummeling.

Dumbbells, a weight bench, and faithful lunchtime pushups during the summer of 1986 had transformed my build. Having finished my freshman year a laughingstock and the brunt of jokes and bullying, I made a commitment to Gold's Gym for the summer. In a few short months, I replaced flabby arms and a gut for some muscles. An iconic moment in my young life happened on my first day back. One of my favorite movies from the eighties was *Can't Buy Me Love*, a story where the geeky Ronald Miller gets the most popular and pretty girl in the high school, Amanda Peterson, to fall for him. My friend, Ashlie Bell (née Marcum), was the title holder of being "Amanda Peterson" at my high school. Ashlie was one of the most well liked and pretty girls in the school, and had always been a good friend to me. Sure, guys choked on their chewing gum when they tried to talk to her, but she never used her looks or popularity to create any drama. Ashlie was a good egg. On that first day of the start of my Sophomore year, she turned to me and said in front of a pretty big crowd of other students in the hallway,

"Wow, Thad! You look really great!" She wasn't just saying that to be nice, as her smile told the truth behind those words. I truly felt better, and looked better, too. My friend had made my day. My month. My high school experience. Anyway, the bullying was over, and my street cred at Dayton Christian High School continued to improve greatly over the next three years.

I would never endure that type of bullying again, but the memories of the beatings, terror, and humiliation of it all will always be with me. I remember saliva hitting my face when they spit on me and the exhaustion of feeling like there wasn't a single thing I could do about it. I was just a kid. I wasn't a fighter, and I handled it the best way I could by simply letting it go. I hated not having many friends, but I always had hoped that one day everything would change. I was glad I was never the bully and that I had always tried to honor God with the way I treated the world around me. I don't know if Ron, Tom, Brook or Rich ever changed or had any regrets for the way they treated me. Whether or not they did, I've forgiven all of those boys. Usually there's something that happened to cause kids to act so hatefully, and I would imagine this was the scenario with everyone who once bullied me. I wondered what darkness might have been lurking in their lives and now hope for them to be free of it all. I didn't have to look very far, though, to find someone else who had faced even more dire scenarios. Jesus faced a battalion of the most vicious bullies this world has ever known.

Jesus had been dragged into court by the angry mob, and almost as soon as they had begun, the trial was over. It was a joke. Jesus was already guilty in their minds, those evil minds belonging to the elders of the people. Darkness had shrouded their reality as the devil had found a way to do something maybe even he thought was impossible. Jesus Christ, the Messiah of all men and women, living, dead and to yet come, had finally been sentenced to hang to his death on a cross. For all appearances, Jesus would not fulfill his role as Savior. Satan was possibly a bit surprised himself at having been able to influence these events more than even he had hoped. From the possession of Judas, to his manipulation of the Pharisees, and everything else that happened around Jesus, the devil's plans were being fulfilled, and Jesus was about to die.

The great brokenness and agony of Jesus must have intensified within him as a battalion of men approached. For years, I just thought a battalion was one small group of soldiers, maybe fifteen men, but I had watched too many movies and was quite wrong. A battalion is anywhere for five to eight hundred men. Imagine the idea of standing alone before five hundred professional soldiers who, as a group, are about to physically take you apart. How do you even reconcile something like this in your mind? Have you ever been overwhelmed physically in such a way that you don't even know how much despair you can handle? That was where Jesus found himself.

This was far worse than a few of the biggest bullies I have encountered. Ron would have been far too small and weak to stand with any of these men. He wasn't vicious enough. These were not sophisticated men who relied on tactical operations to take down their enemy. These were the soldiers of Rome, the most competent, focused, and violent army the world had ever seen. The people cast Jesus to all the brutalities the battalion had to offer.

The battalion began with humiliating Jesus by stripping off all of his clothing. According to Matthew 27, the soldiers next placed a scarlet robe on Jesus and then twisted together a crown of thorns to put onto his head. Next, they mocked him by placing a reed in his hand, emulating a scepter carried by Kings in victories of war. They had brought their disdain and disgust upon Jesus with no sense of any remorse or conscience, and this was just the beginning of what they had planned.

"And they began to salute him, 'Hail, King of the Jews!'" (Mark 15:18)

The battalion of men dropped to their knees in front of him and mocked Jesus with their yells and sneers. One of them took the reed from Jesus' hand and began to strike his head with it while the others spat on him. I have caught myself wondering how long the spitting and beating with the reed continued. Did every soldier get a chance for a blow to the head? Or did they all get to spit in his face?

The power of this moment is completely lost in the words. Our minds cannot wrap themselves around the idea that legions of angels stood by watching as hundreds of men physically tortured and humiliated Jesus. One angel would have been enough to destroy those men in a matter of seconds. In all truth, Jesus himself, with one quick word from his mouth, could have killed everyone in the room. The power of God was within Jesus, yet he did nothing to soften the onslaught of blows. As the reed smashing against his head drove the crown of thorns deeper and deeper, blood began to flow. Jesus endured enormous and terrifying pain. He was probably too weak to raise his hands in defense, let alone even stand up anymore.

It was maybe a year or two earlier that Jesus had met her. She had been bleeding and suffering for twelve years. In late 2015, I went through a weird time where I kept getting these crazy intense nose bleeds. It persisted for about a month and was a constant agitation. I was late to appointments, felt like I was in constant cleanup mode, and made huge messes all around me. Finally, I saw a doctor. They did a little soldering and shocking of the nostril, and after a tiny amount of pain, the bleeding stopped and life went forward. Before the procedure, I had these bloody noses maybe five or six times a week. This lady, however, was bleeding from a discharge for the past twelve years, and I cannot personally fathom anything like this.

Jesus had already shown deep compassion through healing the sick and dying, and this lady was quite aware of who he was and what he could do. Jesus was actually on his way to see a rich man's daughter when she saw him. The daughter had just died, so the father had come to meet Jesus and said, "(If you) come and lay your hand on her, she will live" (Matthew 9:18 author's paraphrase). This man, filled with faith, lead Jesus to his home, but not before the bleeding woman made her way to Jesus through the massive crowd.

"She said to herself, 'If I only touch his garment, I will be made well'" (Matthew 9:21).

She quickly came up behind Jesus, touched his garment, and instantly was healed. "Jesus turned, and seeing her he said, 'Take heart, daughter; your faith has made you well'" (Matthew 9:22).

Next, Jesus followed the rich man to his home and together they moved through the crowd outside of the house. The people had come to mourn, but Jesus was there to do no such thing.

"Go away," he said, "for the girl is not dead but sleeping" (Matthew 9:24, author's paraphrase).

The crowd mocked Jesus and laughed at him, but, honestly, that probably wasn't the first time Jesus was treated that way, and we know it wouldn't be the last time, either. Jesus, though, paid no attention because he was sent to do the work of his Father. He went into the rich man's home and found the daughter. He took the girl by the hand, and when he touched her, she was made well. She got up, and when she did, a fervor erupted, but this time the crowd outside stood rejoicing about the healing and mercy of Jesus.

The mercy of Jesus was evident throughout his ministry, but there was no mercy for him as the battalion struck him again and again. Unbelievably, he was hit in the head with the reed yet another time. Blood and spit covered him, and agony was throbbing throughout his body. The Son of God who had shown compassion and mercy was now being physically destroyed one single heartbreaking blow at a time, and no one was doing anything to slow the merciless attacks against him. Legions of angels stood by, yet no order was given. He had no hope of rescue, but there was no revenge in his heart. Only the will of the Father remained and the determination of Jesus to save us from Hell.

As horrible as the bullying I endured in those three weeks in eighth grade was, it was nothing compared to just a minute of what Jesus endured. I always had hope and believed Ron couldn't kill me or injure me seriously. I could dream of getting away and finally finding the resolve and strength to fight back. When the four boys ran me down, I was outnumbered, but it would have felt entirely different having five hundred bloodthirsty men trying to destroy me. I was never so overwhelmed or bullied to the point that I lost hope. My story was bound to have a better ending, but Jesus already knew where this was all going. He knew the sacrifice he was making and the tenacity and determination it would take to get to the cross.

All I wanted was for Ron and those other boys to leave me alone. If I could have found a gang of my own to fight back with, I would have, but I didn't have a gang. If a teacher or administrator would have been paying some attention, then maybe I would have had a chance to get some relief from the ongoing assaults against me. Jesus could have done anything to change his circumstances, but he chose not to. He was determined to save a sinful and hypocritical people from their just punishment, including even some of the men who were punching, kicking and spitting on him. Was it possible that one of these men at the end of his life would call upon Jesus to save him from an eternity of separation from God?

As each strike connected with Jesus, he was preparing himself for the potential salvation of these very same men. I Timothy 2:4 shares it is the desire of God for everyone to come to salvation through Jesus. Jesus knew the heart of each man and understood more than anyone the struggle some of them may have been facing in that moment. His specific interactions with Peter lead us to the understanding that Jesus knew the future, since he knew the number of times his disciple would betray him. These men had no clue how important they were to Jesus and how his upcoming sacrifice would pave the way to eternal paradise with him.

The soldiers finished torturing Jesus, but they weren't done yet. They thrust the cross upon him and sent him to the streets of Jerusalem. Dragging the wooden beams to his now-certain-doom while his tired and broken body hung together by only a thread, Jesus headed to Calvary. Imagine the scene. Jesus had been tortured and mutilated while being mocked and spat upon. Carrying an inevitable death sentence, he was utterly exhausted pulling the heavy cross and his broken body to the place called Golgotha.

He could have given up. Why didn't Jesus give up? Why didn't he just quit and lie there in the streets and let someone kill him instead of doing all this work just to be executed anyway?

Right there, in that moment, as Jesus was dragging through the streets of Jerusalem the method of death that was destined to take his earthly life, we see an unprecedented amount of determination blasting off of the pages. His will was forged and nothing was going to stop him from following the plans of his Father. The agonizing pain he endured would not stop him. The friends who betrayed him wouldn't make him too demoralized to finish this task. Nothing in this world was going to stop Jesus, and even if Satan understood what he had actually done, he was utterly powerless to stop Jesus. Jesus was tenaciously determined to get to Calvary, and it's the last thing the devil saw coming.

Chapter 12

Nobody Stands Alone

"I didn't find my friends; the good Lord gave them to me."

- Ralph Waldo Emerson

Blood trickled down his dirt and sweat smeared legs. He took another shuffled step. He could barely move, let alone endure the sharp, shooting pain each time his broken body moved a little closer to Calvary. Red splatter was all over his skin and what was left of his clothing. Everything was agony. Jesus struggled to get each foot in front of the next as he somehow bore this cruel tool of his barbaric death, a massive wooden cross, slowly through the streets of Jerusalem. The cross barely clung onto his injured back as he moved down the path. He could simply endure no more and collapsed to the ground in sheer exhaustion. The soldiers seized a man named Simon from the crowd to carry the cross because, physically, Jesus just couldn't take anymore. In all of history, few have suffered such punishment at the hands of men as Jesus did that day.

The cross awkwardly hung on Simon as he and Jesus dragged it through the city streets. The women who knew Jesus mourned while the men looked on in disbelief. Did the other onlookers cheer and rejoice as they had just days earlier on Palm Sunday when Jesus had come into Jerusalem as their Messiah? Or did they jeer and throw angry words at this man who had failed to live up to their fallacious dreams? I imagine most were shocked and sickened at the dehumanization of Jesus into this bloodied and tragic form. How did his angels stomach watching the pulverized and abused Jesus will his way down the desperate road to freedom for all men? Yet this was his purpose. He was almost there.

Throughout my divorce, I often ended up asking God why he allowed the false accusations against me to happen, which, for at least a time, contributed to the loss of so many dear friendships. In the depths of my discouragement, it was nearly impossible for me to pray without asking God, "Why?" What made things even worse was the lack of answers I received while grieving my losses during that time. I didn't see how God was using this trial to make me a more humble, more loving, and more committed follower of Jesus. I didn't understand that even those who were working against God, were still being used by God to execute his plans in my life. God had a purpose and a plan for me, but, in my most haunted and desperate hours, I couldn't see it. I only knew to sit still and trust him.

Jesus, however, had a different purpose and a completely different perspective in his hour of trial. He knew he was fulfilling his Father's will and hundreds of ancient prophecies as he struggled and stumbled down the street while a stranger carried his cross. Even Jesus needed someone to bear part of his load, so God allowed Simon the Cyrene to come along to participate in the final moments before Jesus arrived at the Place of the Skull.

One way or another, the cross had to make its way to Calvary, because God's plans demanded the sacrifice for the world through his only Son, Jesus Christ. When Jesus could no longer carry his cross alone, God made sure Simon was there and was ready. All of Jesus' disciples fled, but God still provided someone to bear his heavy burden in his darkest hour. For a few crucial minutes, God led Simon onto the path of his Savior, and on this harrowing walk in his final moments, Jesus didn't stand alone.

From around 1995 until 2001, I was part of the Generation X ministry at Willowcreek Community Church called Axis. Axis was a community for the after-college crowd who just didn't seem to be able to find their place in a really big church. In the early days, we had to come up with a name for the ministry, and suddenly Axis was born! We wanted to add a little bit of a purpose statement, and after thinking about the community we were trying to create, the words "Nobody Stands Alone" seemed to fit best. We had all recently experienced through our televisions the fighting in Tiananmen Square and had seen one Chinese student standing alone in front of a tank. The tank stopped, as we have all seen countless times. He could have easily run the student over, but the tank didn't move. I imagine the driver of that tank was confused and maybe even thinking to himself, "I do not dare move." This one, young man stood alone in front of a metal monster as the world watched and caught a glimpse of a moment of bravery many of us will never forget.

When we created Axis, we wanted our purpose statement to revolve around the concept that his friends and countrymen should have walked out there with him and also stood in front of the tank. One in front, one on his right, one on his left, and one behind him. The idea of a great community of Christ-followers looks something like this, and this is what the best of the church looks like in our world today.

Some of my friends, however, feel disappointed in the church of today. Some people probably feel a little like

Simon the Cyrene, being grabbed from the safe place where they stand and being forced to carry a burden they didn't want to carry in the first place. Others maybe feel like Peter, great at talking a big game of trusting God in all they would do, but when crisis hits and life gets tough, they run away. They flee and feel like the worst kind of failure. Their failure then festers inside of them and they don't think others can let it go either, so what's the point of trying? The secret truth about our lives as Christians is that we try to live a life free from sin, but we can't. Too often, we run away with our tail between our legs and attempt to hide from those we feel might think less of us. While we should be standing still, getting wrapped up in God's grace and love, we get lost in a sea of good works all gone wrong and are left to pick up the pieces. When we need others the most to provide encouragement, accountability, and strength, we run away from hope into an oblivion of loss and frustration. This is exactly *why* Jesus came, to free us from the burden of sin and death. God never wanted you to walk down the path alone, and he created something so much better for you.

Jesus wasn't alone, though, was he? God had placed a man in his path, Simon the Cyrene. When Simon woke up that morning he probably had no clue he would be carrying the cross of Jesus, the Son of the Almighty God. I'm quite sure he had no idea what this day would bring for him and how his name would go into the annals for all of history for all of time. In this powerful moment, Simon was seized and forced to go stand in front of a tank with Jesus. Not only did he have to carry a cross, but he had to do it in front of all of Jerusalem, and Jerusalem was calling for the death of Jesus the whole way there.

Craig Maxwell was my Simon. He was the person God put in my life to lift some of my burden off of me when I just couldn't carry anymore by myself.

On March 22nd, 2013, Craig sent me a quick message. It started out, "Hey Thad. Thought of you today." It's funny how small some of these things happen, isn't it? Maybe funny isn't the word. Maybe God-ordained is more fitting.

I had been living with my Mom for about a week in her Senior Living Apartment. As false allegations came against me, my world was now filled with interrogations and skepticism from my church leaders and some of my closest friends. My Mom stood by me, though, and always believed the best in me. I walked down a devastatingly broken path and quickly realized I felt very alone. Even my closest friends from church battled against doubt and wondered out loud to me in this mess if the allegations would be proved true. The one person who was maybe my closest friend at the time simply disappeared. He didn't return my calls and only responded to a couple of emails. I realized I was standing face-to-face with a tank and it felt like I was standing there completely alone. There had been low points in my life, but nothing compared to being mired in this deep tragedy of betrayals and lies.

I didn't know how to respond to Craig. Maybe I shouldn't, I thought. Did I really need another person judging me? Did I really need someone to tell me what to do, or someone else screaming at me to repent? Did I really need someone else wanting answers to all of these horrible questions? It was weird, but for some reason the Lord led me to spill my very painful story to my old friend, Craig.

I shared with him a few pieces of my story and he wanted to meet for breakfast immediately, like the next morning. I was broke, but found enough cash to pay for the gas to get there. It's funny, but Craig actually bought me breakfast, without even knowing I didn't have enough money. He seemed to know exactly what I needed. He listened, encouraged me in prayer and through the scriptures, and always seemed to know what to say to comfort my devastated heart. Craig became a very trusted friend, someone I could count on for truth and guidance. With his permission, I'll share the response my friend sent me after I recounted with him some good things the Lord was doing, as well as some challenges I was facing, specifically feeling so discouraged by the balloons of doubt that kept swelling up all around me -

Thad,

Thanks for sharing. When the other prefects tried to find skeletons in Daniel's closet they could not find anything, no bad business practices, no pornography, no sexual immorality, no drunkenness, nothing!!! He was squeaky clean, above reproach. The only way they could find wrong doing was to create new laws involving Daniel's God. They knew he would remain consistent and keep his integrity. May we be the kind of men that can only be found guilty as a result of our commitment to remain above reproach and consistently follow God and his Word. Remain a man of integrity my friend, scripture tells us and demonstrates that God will reward you for it. Thanks for this encouraging note, I am praying for you!

Craig was referring to Daniel from the Old Testament. Daniel lived around six hundred years before Jesus and was a top official for King Darius. Several of the other officials in the kingdom were jealous of Daniel, so they schemed and planned to destroy him before the king. As hard as they tried, every attempt they made failed. Daniel was an impossible man for them to deal with because he refused to be corrupted. Just like Craig wrote, they had to try to destroy him in the only way they could, by forcing him to choose between obeying the laws of men or obeying the laws of God. They knew Daniel would choose God, and their shrewdness seemed to pay off. They caught Daniel red handed choosing to disobey the new laws put forward and went to the king immediately with their proof.

King Darius realized he had been tricked by his officials, but he was forced to obey the laws he had just put in place. The king did everything he could to save Daniel, but nothing he tried worked. He had to obey his new law, so Daniel was sent to be destroyed by the lions. From the book of Daniel, chapter six, verse 16, we see the king bless Daniel, saying, "May your God, whom you serve continually, rescue you!"

The stone was placed over the mouth of the den. Daniel was alone in the darkness with monsters. Or was he?

Anguish filled the heart of the king in the wee hours of a sleepless night. The lions would have made quick work of Daniel, most likely tearing through him in a matter of seconds. There was no way out, and no man could save him. After a seemingly endless night for the king, the sun finally rose and King Darius sprinted to the lion's den. The stone remained in place, and the light shone into the darkness as they removed it, exposing the hole Daniel had been cast into.

> As he came near to the den where Daniel was, he cried out in a tone of anguish. The king

declared to Daniel, "O Daniel, servant of the living God, has your God, whom you serve continually, been able to deliver you from the lions?" Then Daniel said to the king, "O king, live forever! My God sent his angel and he shut the lions' mouths, and they have not harmed me, because I was found blameless before him; and also before you, O king, I have done no harm." Then the king was exceedingly glad, and commanded that Daniel be taken up out of the den. So Daniel was taken up out of the den, and no kind of harm was found on him, because he had trusted in his God (Daniel 6:20-23).

Daniel was set up and personally attacked by men who probably acted like his friends. They even had him tossed alone into the lion's den. Daniel, however, trusted the living God, and God knew Daniel needed his help. He knows all of our needs! God sent an angel to stay with Daniel and protect him from the mouths of the vicious lions. When I was falsely accused, God sent my friend Craig to believe in me and to be there in the darkest part of a painful tribulation. After Jesus was falsely accused and convicted, our Heavenly Father sent Simon the Cyrene to be on the path to Calvary so he could carry the cross when Jesus was simply too broken to carry it by himself. God knows exactly what we need, and he sends help at the perfect time. The scriptures show us this, and Daniel in the Lion's Den and Jesus on the road to Calvary are just two of hundreds of examples.

There are many in the church today, like Simon, who have reached down and picked up a burden that was too heavy for someone to carry on their own. God destined Simon, Daniel's angel, and my friend Craig to be there for those who love God so they could survive the trials, tribulations, and nightmares of this too often cruel world. God is faithful and will provide for us, especially when we need him the most. Simon didn't have a clue, but two thousand years later he is still known as the man who carried the cross of God's only Son. What an amazing connection for one man to have with Jesus, and it's in these connections God may be using you right now.

The truth is, it's inevitable that one day you will be like Daniel, tossed into a lion's den and having done nothing to deserve it. You will be blind in the darkness, and there will be a horrible, low growling as the lions threaten to destroy you. Then everything will change in an instant as a new light shines upon you and the lions no longer make any noise. You will know you are not alone and that there is protection sent by the God of the Heavens Himself. It will still be a long night in the darkness, but you will be safe and you will definitely not alone.

Some day you will have the chance to be like my good friend Craig. You'll get a message from a broken and hurting friend who will need a little encouragement and hope in their life. They might have really screwed up, or maybe they will be dealing with the resulting consequences in a situation that isn't their fault, but either way, God will have brought them to you and there has to be a reason.

There will also be a day when you will be grabbed out of nowhere, like Simon the Cyrene and there will be no choice but to carry the entire burden of someone else. It wouldn't have started as your burden at all, but you won't be able to walk away and just leave them alone. Whatever the circumstances, it will now be yours, too, and somehow you'll need to stay with them and see this thing to the end. God will have to help you, though, because we can't do these things on our own.

The angel followed the direct orders of God the Father and was sent directly into the lion's den to protect Daniel. Be brave my friends! Even if you are chosen to be the one to shut the mouths of lions, God will protect you. Simon was seized and carried the cross of Jesus Christ to Calvary. He was chosen to bear the burden, and he stayed with Jesus until the very end of their road together. Craig showed great empathy and listened to the great woes of a sorrowful and broken man. He could have been a part of so many other's lives, but chose to stay with me to deliver truth and encouragement from God's word. The angel, Simon, and Craig each played a unique role in God's plans to help bear or even completely remove the burdens of someone else.

As Jesus got closer and closer to Calvary, he prepared to sacrifice everything for the sake of this world. Not only did he set our ultimate example of obedience to the Father, but he demonstrated the tenacity, empathy, and love that moved his broken body all the way up the Mount of Calvary. More than anything, it was his love for God and his love for us that perpetuated the final steps of this journey before his crucifixion. The love of Jesus was about to be on full display for Jerusalem, the dark powers of this world, the heavenly host, and for all of men until the end of time.

Chapter 13

Sacrifice

"He is no fool who gives what he cannot keep to gain that which he cannot lose."

- Jim Elliot

He is a hair taller than most, with an average build, and after a couple of decades in Tennessee, his Southern accent still isn't quite fully developed. He built almost all of their beautiful home with his own two hands. His old, dark green pickup truck whizzes by with a huge American Flag decal over the back window, though not by his choice. A family member put it there, so he left it, though I'm not sure if he really wanted it. He tinkers with that pickup and somehow keeps it running long after a mechanical idiot like myself would have been able to keep it on the road. He is a quiet, intelligent, blue-collared guy with a calm demeanor and a ton of selflessness built in. You'd have to know him pretty well to discover how smart and well read this country boy of ours really is. He tries to keep surprises to a minimum because he never likes them himself. He also doesn't care much for clowns or hippos.

I first met J.R. Gwartney in early 2003 when my family and I moved to Jackson, Tennessee. His wife, Amy, is his perfect match, as she understands the unique gifts her husband possesses. J.R. is one of those amazing people who helps others in almost any way possible. He is known for pulling over to help stranded motorists, and then has more than a few stories to share about it. There are countless people he has helped, so many that I'm not sure there is a single person he ever met whom he hasn't majorly gone out of his way for in some way. J.R. doesn't serve others so he can have a fun story to share, though. He does it because he genuinely cares about and greatly values people.

Sometimes much to his family's dismay.

"You shouldn't give him your kidney. What if I need it???" exclaimed one of J.R.'s relatives, indignantly, after he announced his intentions of donating one of his kidneys.

"Well, I have an extra kidney, so I guess he can have one of mine," J.R. told me one afternoon from his porch. J.R. had heard about a man at work who needed a kidney, so he decided the best thing to do was to give him one of his. He didn't really know the man, and, if memory serves, I think J.R. had only been in his presence only once or twice before. Regardless, this man needed a kidney and J.R. was a perfect match, so he decided that's just what he'd do. When his friends and family heard about it, there were a ton of questions, but truthfully I don't think any of us were really surprised.

There was an article written about J.R. at his company, which is one of the largest companies in the world, and a lot of coworkers responded with admiration and enthusiasm around what he had done. I can imagine J.R. sitting there shaking his head and telling them it wasn't that big of a deal, and he didn't really need his story to be told publicly. My friend simply preferred the man have a working kidney without any of the fanfare. I personally laugh a good bit when I think of my humble friend trying to answer all those questions everyone kept asking him. He was never one to seek attention.

Giving someone you don't know your kidney is a pretty amazing sacrifice to make. Truthfully, giving a kidney to someone you care deeply about is still a pretty amazing sacrifice. I'm not sure how such a thing is actually done, but I would truly like to keep both of mine. In fact, my kidneys feel a little weird right now as I am thinking about this. In the meantime, J.R. probably wishes he was born with three kidneys just to give one more away.

In August of 2009, I wasn't doing well. Out of nowhere, I was thrown onto an emotional roller coaster as the nauseating tension kept churning constantly in the pit of my stomach from the stress of my first marriage suddenly becoming very rocky. I was hurt and confused by some of the words and actions of others in my life, especially a few of the people I trusted the most. My heart was exhausted from the potential loss of my marriage. I needed to feel some peace in my life again. I needed to do something about these horrible feelings haunting me day and night. I realized what I really needed, though, was to see my friend J.R., so I jumped in my car and drove to Jackson, Tennessee. I was struggling with my identity, self-confidence and these crazy, turbulent emotions, and when I needed a friend, I called on the one guy I knew who would speak the truth and love to me better than anyone else. His wife, Amy, is no slouch either, always willingly devoting her gifts, love, and time to others. She opened her home, cooked me up some great food, and listened intently while providing wisdom and encouragement. He and Amy have always been the most welcoming and warm people I have known, and I am blessed to call them my friends.

What makes my friend, J.R., special is the way he serves others. First of all, it's often random. He doesn't only help folks with a broken down car. He fixes their washers or dryers and assorted other appliances. Yet his life's calling isn't to just fix things, but rather to be a great encourager. My friend isn't afraid to tell people where they need some work, but in the same breath tells them what they are doing well. There are few others with such a gift of service like my friend, J.R. Sacrificing his kidney is just the tip of the iceberg when we look at a man who built a world around him through his love and selflessness. JR also manages to help those who could never help him back. He always seems to find the people who need him most, provides some help and encouragement, and then he is gone before you can thank him. My friend truly understands the sacrifice of Jesus and is a living, breathing example of such an amazing thing.

The love and sacrifice of Jesus lives today in the lives of those who love, know and obey him. This isn't just having the car in front of you pay for your drink at Starbucks. These are people like the two Jason's who run BOGG Ministries out of Miamisburg, Ohio. BOGG is a mobile food pantry, enlisting the help of individuals and churches throughout the Dayton area to help spread God's goodness to everyone who gets in line for a little love and a lot of food. It can also be found in friends of mine like Bob and Debi Cowan who are sharing Jesus with the people of Roatan, Honduras by teaching them a skill they can use to provide for their families and helping them understand how much God loves them. Their shop is called Made-In-Roatan, and they are using their business as a ministry to lead the people of Roatan out of poverty and out of a spiritual darkness. Loving and serving the world around us isn't a unique calling, but it does require a good amount of courage. One night, in those dark days of 2013, someone found their courage and came to me with a little hope and love when I needed it most.

My head was hung lower than low as I trudged slowly down the aisle to the front. The pastor had told us to come forward if we needed prayer, and I was a total train wreck on this Saturday night. Everything around me felt so very broken, like my world was crushing in on me. Nothing really made sense, but he said they would pray, and the idea of having others praying for me seemed to give me a little comfort. I probably looked like a disaster shuffling down the long aisle, but fortunately, the area in front of the stage was pretty busy with a lot of other folks, maybe some like me.

I got down on my knees and soon there were three different hands on my back. A few minutes later, the pastor closed us in prayer and I stood up and recognized two of those hands as two friends of mine who gave me an encouraging nod and a hearty handshake. I smiled as best I could. One of them said he'd call me that week. It was good. I was grateful.

But then something very different happened. My two friends headed back to their seats and now the third hand that had been touching my back made herself known. I had no clue who she was, but I'll remember what happened next for the rest of my life.

She was about half my age and about half my size. She smiled and looked right into me. Dead into me. There was a particular strength in those eyes as she reached forward and embraced my hands in hers.

"Is it ok if I hold your hands?"

"Sure," I whispered.

Everything slowed down and the thousand people around us disappeared. Tears started forming in my eyes, but I wasn't going to cry, was I? Her powerful gaze continued as she began to speak.

"I'm Melissa. I know I don't know you but God sent me up here to tell you that He loves you. I'm supposed to tell you that He loves you very, very much. He is with you through everything you're going through right now. I am absolutely certain He wants me to tell you this, so I wanted to let you know."

It got real small real fast right there. Real small. The young lady securely gripped my hands in both of hers as we spoke. She looked me straight in the eye and she wanted to make sure I understood every single word she said. I wanted to say something, but I couldn't speak. I didn't know what to say. I almost started crying, but I was just too stunned to let the tears out.

I think I muttered thanks, but I just don't know. I don't know. I can remember verbatim what she said, but I have no clue what happened after that. I always seem to be able to remember these moments, but that night, as I sat down to write about it all, I remembered nothing after she walked away. All I knew was she was gone and I was headed back to my seat.

It makes sense why Jesus said in Matthew 12:50, "For whoever does the will of my Father in heaven is my brother and sister and mother." In that moment, the young lady and I were family, and she was sent by our Father to care for and encourage me. A new hope and love enveloped me as God began to cover all of my hurt and wounds in this and with more encouraging moments that were to come. It seemed so surreal, almost as if God had sent an angel to come to me, as he did for Jesus after he left Satan in the desert.

The memories of this moment and the angel disguised as a college girl still leave me in awe of the goodness of God's love for me, and for all of us. I don't know if I'll ever see that young lady again outside of heaven, but it's pretty cool to have that moment etched in my memory for the rest of my life. I always believed God would be there for me, and when I experienced something so deeply encouraging, it brought me a ton of peace and feelings of being valued and loved by my God. In that brave girl's sacrifice of herself for a potentially awkward moment, she approached a stranger and showed me a sisterly type of love and a goodness when I was so desperate for just a little hope.

There are many today in our world who believe Jesus' sacrifice for us requires more than just some lukewarm emotional understanding. They are the ones who understand the sacrifice Jesus made and what it meant to the world, and it's the reason they raise money for the journey into foreign countries to share God's message of love and hope to an unreached people. Or they reject our culture's materialistic bent and give money to those who are giving their life to help the poor. Maybe time is what they give to Jesus, deciding they aren't too busy to take in a hurting man from Ohio into their beautiful Tennessee home. For all of them, they've received a new purpose and peace from God that makes them operate in this life in a completely different way than most others. Jesus is the leader of the lives of J.R., the two Jason's, the Cowan's, and the mystery college girl/angel, and it's quite obvious they are all very different people than most of us encounter every day. When I talk to them, I think of Jesus, because no one ever understood what sacrifice truly meant more than him.

Jesus was almost to Calvary, also called The Skull. Every move he made, every stuttered step as he somehow kept his feet under him, was done out of love for you and me. He finally reached the summit of the hill where he was to hang upon that horrible cross and to endure more unrelenting, ruthless agony than you and I can imagine. They took a nail and hammered it through his left hand and another through his right. His hands were torn, but kept intact just enough so he could hold himself up. By spreading his hands on opposite sides of the cross, Jesus had to lift his body weight up until he eventually couldn't hold it up anymore, and when he couldn't, he would no longer be able to fill his lungs with air. Nails were also pounded through his feet, and there was no rest or relief to be found in this new pain.

The crown of thorns was stuck violently on his head. The sign that was hung above his torn and broken body mocked him, bearing the words, "This is the King of the Jews." He was probably still drenched in the spit of the soldiers, and taunts persist from every side.

"If you are the King of the Jews, save yourself!" (Luke 23:37) the soldiers screamed and laughed as the cross was thrust into the ground, his body jerking as he was hung.

Maybe the Pharisees still wondered if he might do another one of his miracles. Maybe Satan was waiting to see if legions of angels would show up and pull him off of the cross. Maybe the people were starting to wonder if this was really what they wanted and if Jesus was going to come down and fight for his life. If any of them thought there would be a war or revenge, they were wrong. Love still ruled.

"Father, forgive them, for they know not what they do," (Luke 23:34) an exhausted and broken Jesus said as he fought for some air to reach his lungs.

No one would have suspected such an open handed and undeniably compassionate moment of forgiveness in such a brutal setting. If anyone ever had the right to be angry at someone, it was Jesus. Jesus, though, is the best example of resisting bitterness and revenge. He shows us, even in an extremely painful and humiliating death, the most beautiful demonstration of love and grace.

Jesus wasn't the only man on a cross that day. On both his right and his left were criminals sentenced to die with Jesus. They had been found guilty of crimes against humanity, and were now paying the ultimate price for their deeds.

"One of the criminals who were hanged railed at him, saying, 'Are you not the Christ? Save yourself and us!' But the other rebuked him, saying, 'Do you not fear God, since you are under the same condemnation? And we indeed justly, for we are receiving the due reward of our deeds; but this man has done nothing wrong! Jesus remember me when you come into your kingdom'" (Luke 23:39-42).

Jesus said to the man, "Truly, I say to you, today you will be with me in paradise" (Luke 23:43).

Even on the cross, the compassion of Jesus was unlike anyone else in the history of our world. Remember, his hands were nailed to a cross, along with his feet. He was very likely hanging naked before all of Jerusalem, including both men and women. The blood and spit that had covered him earlier had now dried, as the gashes from the whips and the reed he was beaten with still ached deep in whatever flesh still remained. His disciples had fled, the women who followed him sobbed, and his final breath was merely moments away.

His mom, Mary, was there. She had her sister and Mary Magdalene standing there in the middle of this excruciating nightmare. His mother was with him from his birth, and now she watched him suffer in agony. John, his disciple, and one of his closest friends, was also there.

Jesus saw John and his mother together and shouted to Mary, "Woman, behold your son!" (John 19:26).

And to John he said, "Behold, your mother!" (John 19:27).

John took Mary home with him on that day and cared for her as if she was his own mother. Jesus knew the love and gratefulness that flowed in the heart of John, and he knew how passionately John had followed him. John's motives were pure, and Jesus knew he would be the one to best care for his Mom after such an ugly and heart-wrenching day.

The chief priests and others who were the type of people that might enjoy watching men die were now at The Place of the Skull to insult, mock, and taunt Jesus one final time. Jesus may have been nailed to the cross, but he was never helpless. It is incredibly important to remember that Jesus always remained the Son of God and could have saved himself at any time. It was his choice to suffer and to die willingly, and he did it so he could save us from our sins.

"And those who passed by derided him, wagging their heads and saying, 'Aha! You who would destroy the temple and rebuild it in three days, save yourself, and come down from the cross'" (Mark 15:29-30).

The chief priests and scribes then also mocked Jesus saying, "He saved others; he cannot save himself. He is the King of Israel; let him come down now from the cross, and we will believe in him" (Matthew 27:42).

It was early, but a deep darkness fell over all of the land. *"The sun's light had failed" (Luke 23:45).* "And when the sixth hour had come, there was darkness over the whole land until the ninth hour" (Mark 15:33).

As the darkness stole the light, and hope faded for many, Jesus suddenly called out with a loud voice, "My God, my God, why have you forsaken me?" (Matthew 27:46).

Psalm chapter twenty-two was written by King David, and his life was in shambles more often than probably anyone else I've ever known or studied. He had a king throw a spear at him. He had a man killed in battle so he could take the man's wife, then he slept with her, despite the fact they were both married to other people, and got her pregnant. He then had to watch as his son tragically died. He was chased out of his kingdom by one of his kids and lived a very strange life to the end of his days. Even through all of this, God still loved David and David greatly loved God. In his darkest and most perilous moments, he cried out to God and God answered him. As death now overwhelmed him, Jesus quoted King David from Psalm twenty-two, breathed his last breath, and then something miraculous happened in the temple.

"Then Jesus, calling out with a loud voice, said, 'Father, into your hands I commit my spirit!' And having said this he breathed his last" (Luke 23:46).

"And behold, the curtain of the temple was torn in two, from top to bottom. And the earth shook, and the rocks were split" (Matthew 27:51).

For thousands of years, the Temple Curtain stood as the physical barrier between God and man. The only way for man to actually be with God was for the High Priest to enter through the curtain alone into the Holy of Holies. The curtain represented not only the way to God the Father, but it also represented the space between us and God. As the followers of God would go to the temple to worship him, the curtain was always there and the presence of God was just on the other side. In the moment Jesus cried out in his death, the curtain was torn and there was no more space between God and man.

Sin did this to us. Sin had separated us from God the Father.

"But your iniquities (sins) have made a separation between you and your God, and your sins have hidden his face from you so that he does not hear" (Isaiah 59:2).

The curtain not only established the path to direct access to God the Father, but it also established a true separation between us and God. Without understanding the distinct separation between us and God, we cannot understand the need to repent and the need for Jesus to save us.

Some archaeologists and historians believe the curtain in the temple could have been up to four inches thick! I can't even wrap my mind around a massive, four inch thick curtain. Sin can feel unbelievably overwhelming, too, can't it? Addictions to pornography can be paralyzing, and lust can often become the burden of a secret sin many have given up fighting to overcome. The desire to control and manipulate others to get what we want can dominate our lives to the point where only true accountability and repentance, and God's grace of course, can save us. When we create a lifestyle of sin, we can't do a thing about changing it without Jesus' blood and God's forgiveness and grace. With true repentance and a deep understanding of what Jesus did for us on the cross, we can begin to experience God's grace and a new life, and this all happens because of Jesus.

The death of Jesus on the cross changed everything. When the curtain was torn, the space between man and God was removed, giving birth to a new freedom for us to experience a personal relationship with God. What was once a barrier has been transformed into The Way, and The Way is Jesus.

As the curtain was rent from top to bottom, the world was blanketed in complete and total darkness. There was no eclipse or some other random atmospheric event. There was more going on here than the people of Israel, or for that matter anyone on our planet, could understand.

"He (Jesus) himself bore our sins in his body on the tree, that we might die to sin and live to righteousness" (1 Peter 2:24).

No one else could do this. No one else was ever going to be able to sacrifice themselves for us the way Jesus did. Jesus was the only human in history with such raw holiness and power over sin. In that moment, the sinless Jesus took the sin and darkness of the entire world upon himself, causing the curtain to tear and creating a path directly to God.

Lust. Greed. Murder. Rape. Lying. Hate. Cheating. Stealing. Malice. Adultery. Abuse. Jesus died experiencing and absorbing your sins being put on him by God the Father. Jesus died experiencing and absorbing all of *my* sins, too. It was more, though, than our sins and our deeds. It was everyone who had ever sinned and everyone who would one day desire to surrender their will, mind, and heart to him.

It's almost impossible to envision how Jesus could suddenly have a world of darkness and sin cast on him all at once. His last moments before he died were inheriting the mind numbing, heartbreaking and disgusting sins of a world that needs Jesus today more than ever. The good news is Jesus did this willingly. He pursued this moment and was tenacious in seeing this through to the end. He knew what was about to happen, but still, he kept going. He knew he was going to experience a darkness like no one else ever had or ever will, but he remained on the cross until it was over. I can't imagine the horror of the burden Jesus took upon himself in that moment, and frankly, I don't think any of us really can or would want to. The sacrifice of Jesus Christ wasn't just a physical sacrifice. As he took upon himself all of the darkness of humanity, an emotional, mental, and spiritual death broke him like no one else would ever be broken. How do we understand something like this? How do we reconcile that every sinful action and every sinful thought of everyone who ever drew breath was willingly placed onto Jesus, God's innocent Son, who was nailed to a cross. Jesus knew everything, he experienced all of sin, and he died a death we deserved. Every action in his life led to that moment where he would suffer and die by being crucified on a cross on hill just outside of Jerusalem.

Ruthlessly stabbing his side, the soldiers confirmed the death of Jesus. Water flowed out of him and onto the ground below. The Pharisees and others left The Place of the Skull, going to their homes to, of all things, somehow prepare for the Sabbath (the Jewish day of rest). They laughed loudly, boasting of what they did and how the "imposter" could not save himself. Others in the crowd were silent, just taking in the shocking, barbaric, and horrifying moment. I can't imagine the heartbreak of his mother. Unlike anyone else, she had experienced all thirty-three years of the goodness and love of Jesus, and now she watched helplessly as his body was utterly destroyed.

With holes in his hands, a crown of thorns still crushed onto his head, wounds on his feet, side and, frankly, all over his body, Jesus was finally brought down from the cross and taken to be placed in a tomb. John took an exhausted and broken Mary home to care for her. Peter was in mourning and heartbroken over his three very recent denials of being a follower of Jesus. The other disciples were scattered, hiding, leaderless, and confused. Hope was fleeting, and those who loved him were left with memories, a lot of questions, and the brutal and haunting scene of the cross.

But a new light was about to carve its way through the darkness as a somber spirit settled over Jerusalem. Some, including the devil, were rejoicing, but they wouldn't be when they figured out what was really going on. No, this wasn't the end of Jesus' story, and the devil would soon realize what he had actually done. The light of the world was not about to stay buried, and the power of Jesus was going to bring him back to life.

Chapter 14

Darkness and Light

"Only in the darkness can you see the stars."

- Martin Luther King, Jr.

"It was now about the sixth hour, and there was darkness over the whole land until the ninth hour, while the sun's light failed" (Luke 23:44-45).

I didn't want to be a cowboy this year. I wasn't some little kid anymore. Cowboy costumes were for babies, and it was time for this eight year old to become something better, something that would make this the greatest Halloween of my very young life. Mom and I talked a lot about it and we finally made the best decision possible. I was going as a Luke Skywalker with a green lightsabre (best color EVER for a lightsabre), oversized robe and everything! In the world of boys, this was an epic decision, and one that would greatly impact my street cred. And there was always the possibility if I held out my hand, and focused hard enough, I might just be able to make something move. I mean, seriously, what little boy didn't check to see if they had Jedi powers?

Mom and I headed out into our neighborhood right when it started getting dark. The year was 1980 and we lived in Wheaton, Illinois, a place that felt like the safest small town in America. I licked my lips in the wild fantasy of pouring out a mountain of Three Musketeers bars, M&M's, and Reese's Peanut Butter Cups from my makeshift goody bag, which, of course, was the pillowcase from my NFL bed sheets. There would be no erasers or the always-dreaded pencils this year! It felt more like a perfect summer night, going from house to house, as friendly neighbors dropped my favorite candy and so much more in my bag. There was even one apple, because there was always one apple, and I didn't mind as long as it didn't have a razor blade inside. Mom said somebody got a razor blade in an apple on Halloween once, which didn't make sense. If you're giving apples out on Halloween, you're the only one in your neighborhood doing it, and you're going to be easily identified, you'll go to prison, and everyone will hate you. Logic, however, is not a requirement for eight year old boys, and I had no problem staying away from fruit on Halloween!

We'd been ringing neighbors doorbells for about an hour and it had gotten pretty dark. Mom and I embarked on our small journey a little later than most of my friends around the neighborhood, so almost all of the kids had disappeared into their houses for the night. It was pretty quiet when my Mom saw one of her friends. This was definitely not the time for her to stop to have a conversation, interrupting the precious few moments I had left. My bag didn't have nearly enough candy inside. My goals were in danger of not being met, and my patience was growing thin. How could Mom be talking to her friend while we were trick or treating? I needed to get moving as quickly as possible.

Mom sensed my impatience, looked at me and said, "Why don't you just go a few houses up ahead. I'll be here for just a few more minutes and I'll catch up to you. Or, if you finish the block, just come back and get me."

She didn't need to tell me twice, and I was already running across the street as she yelled behind me, "You make sure you look both ways the next time you cross!"

Mom was always talking to me about being more careful, but this was not an easy thing for a rambunctious boy in hot pursuit of Halloween candy. At three years old, I terrified my neighbors by learning how to ride a two wheel bike, mostly striking fear in their hearts because of my crazy, fast speed for such a little kid. Adults kept telling me to slow down, but there was no way I was going to. Going fast was too much fun. I raced everywhere I could, while wrecking far more often than I care to remember. My body is still littered with scars from my bike and skateboard wrecks from my childhood, and I think I was probably just a little too big and clumsy to ride the way I did. It was a lot of fun, though.

Time was ticking away and I needed to hit these houses fast. I landed on the next porch, but realized when I got to the door every light, including the one on the front porch, was turned out. We never rang the doorbell if there weren't any lights on, and with little time left to get candy now, I wasn't messing around. I quickly walked away and headed to the next house.

It was very dark, and with no lights on in the house, it felt pitch black as I began to walk through their yard. I dodged a few pine trees as I cut through the grass, walking towards the next house. Turning back for a quick glance, I could barely see Mom way off in the distance now, still on the neighbor's porch talking to her friend. There was no point in waving, since it was so dark where I stood. She wouldn't be able to see me anyway. She could probably hear me if I yelled, but the street was empty, and she knew I was heading out of her sight for a few minutes. I turned back, and began to head again towards the next house, but suddenly fear overwhelmed me as I felt something wrap around my neck. There was no point struggling. They had me and were dragging me into the darkness.

Without a doubt, I was completely overpowered. Identifying the object around my neck as a thick chain, they used that and their hands to forcefully move me away from the light. Most of the force, however, was coming from the person with that chain around my neck, and I quickly grabbed a hold of it to alleviate the intense choking. Dread shot through me as, from what I could see, there were three of them. I was now clearly out of sight of my mother, blocked by a large pine tree on the side yard. Even though I was only a few feet out of sight, she had absolutely no view of where I was.

Suddenly, they stopped dragging me and stood me up. They were taller than me, but not quite the size of adults. All three of them were wearing the most frightening masks I had ever seen. One of them stood behind me with the metal chain wrapped tight around my neck. The other two stood there in front of me with those hideous faces, just staring at me as I struggled. We had a couple of pretty rough high school kids in our neighborhood, but I knew to stay away from them. I had been out on my bike when they called me over once. They lured me into a dark garage, grabbed me and began to shove me back and forth between them. Next, they spit on me, but before it got any worse, I broke through the circle and grabbed my bike. I rode away as fast as I could, never looking back. It was fairly traumatic, but I got away and wasn't hurt.

I couldn't understand what the two masked figures were waiting for as I was still standing there, but suddenly I wasn't. The masked assailant behind me brutally kicked my legs out from under me and now I was hanging by the chain around my neck. He seemed quite strong and able to handle me as I fought tooth and nail to support myself, my fingers clenched, grabbing onto the chain. I was somewhat successful, but still being slowly choked. One of them had grabbed my bag of candy and tossed it on the ground nearby. Breathing was starting to get difficult, and there was no way I could yell for my mom. They whispered threats of what they would do if I called out for her. They said they would kill me, and I believed them.

Fear swept through me more and more by the second. I didn't know how this would go and if they were planning to kill me, but thankfully the moment only lasted for a few seconds. I knew if I was going to get out of this, I needed to do something fast, and the longer I didn't fight back, the more likely I'd be seriously hurt or worse. As fast and hard as I possibly could, I threw every elbow and kick I could behind me at the kid with the chain wrapped around my neck. He must not have been ready because he quickly went down, and I was free from the chain and could breathe again. Without hesitating a second, I screamed for my mom, grabbed my bag of candy, and sprinted towards the street light. Mom was right where I left her. Somehow I had escaped and had not lost a single piece of candy.

The next day, my neighbor said a high school kid was mugged not far from where I was grabbed. He told me the other victim was beaten up bad enough to go to the hospital. I saw him about a week later with two of the worst black eyes I had ever seen. He said it was three masked guys who mugged him, and they were quite vicious. I knew the Lord had taken care of me, but it was still a very frightening situation to have endured.

Over time, as we mature, our fears change and adjust. Our lives open up to an even bigger world, and we are faced with different kinds of threats. I would encounter terror again more than twenty years later, but this time it was on my television when a group of terrorists hijacked planes full of people.

The planes were flying at least five hundred miles an hour when they hit the towers. September 11th, 2001 changed our lives and our world forever. Most of us will never forget where we were as we watched those planes destroy tons of metal and an unfathomable number of lives. I came around the corner and into our breakroom at work just in time to see on TV the second plane fly into the building. I watched as pockets of smoke and fire burst through the steel structure.

The two towers of the World Trade Center came down just moments apart and, when they did, terror and chaos erupted throughout all of New York City. Human lives were falling out of the sky above them, as New Yorkers looked on in disbelief and tearful sadness. The final fall of each tower was concentrated; they dropped sickeningly straight down, destroying their foundations thoroughly. Shock waves from the fall of both towers were felt up to forty miles away, while the world watched in utter horror on almost every channel in every country.

My mind was racing. Where were my children and were they okay? After calling home and finding out everyone was just fine, I went back to the TV and stared at the screen. Slowly, reality set in and there was anger, yes, but a deep and overwhelming sadness filled my heart. If faced with the nightmare choice of burning to death or jumping from a thousand feet, what would you choose?

On 9/11 many fathers, mothers, sisters, and brothers had to make choices like this, or much worse.

On September 17th, Late Night TV host David Letterman returned to his show for what many refer to as the most important words spoken about what happened on 9/11. There was some anticipation of hearing him speak to us on that night because we knew he would help us begin to understand how to process all of this. This is a portion of the transcript –

> It's terribly sad here in New York City. We've lost five thousand fellow New Yorkers, and you can feel it. You can feel it. You can see it. It's terribly sad. Terribly, terribly sad. The reason we were attacked, the reason these people are dead, these people are missing and dead, and they weren't doing anything wrong, they were living their lives, they were going to work, they were traveling, they were doing what they normally do. As I understand it (and my understanding of this is vague at best), another smaller group of people stole some airplanes and crashed them into buildings. And we're told that they were zealots, fueled by religious fervor… religious fervor. And if you live to be a thousand years old, will that make any sense to you? We're going to try and feel our way through this, and we'll just see how it goes… take it a day at a time.

Sadness washed over all of us as we wished we could turn off the TV and make everything go back to the way it was before 8:46 am on September 11th. We couldn't watch the coverage without tears, pointing at the television, or gasping at the terror in front of us. The horror of watching moms and dads, sons and daughters, brothers and sisters, and best friends falling to their deaths was too much for most of us to comprehend.

We knew these actions were a direct and hostile shot at our hearts, an attempt to destroy our sense of trust and security. We were confused and didn't know how to feel about this real-life-nightmare. We didn't know how or if we would ever move forward into something good again. Everything was placed on pause and we just sat in the ashes and memories for awhile.

It felt like evil had won something on September 11th. The loss of life was like a vacuum sucking all the spirit out of our insides, leaving us shocked and empty. We turned televisions on and off and on and off, unsure morally what we were supposed to do. Do we look again? Should we watch this nightmare played out on a screen, or do we just try to move past it, as though something else would help us to recover, to heal, and maybe somehow we could just forget.

Most of us weren't anywhere near the World Trade Center, The Pentagon, or that field in Pennsylvania that day, but it was almost as if we all experienced the same anguish as we watched from so far away. Maybe we needed to see the humanness of it all and watch the agony of what the victims suffered. Maybe we were hoping for a hero to ride in and do something, anything, to right this wrong, but how could anyone combat so much destruction to save so many lives? Personally, I couldn't process it. The permanence of the moment wasn't lost on me in the shock of what happened. I wasn't thinking about our response or justice. I was, probably just like you, overwhelmed with grief.

As our world dramatically changed from the events of 9/11, imagine the shock and sadness around the disciples and the women that loved and followed Jesus as complete darkness settled over the land. Slowly, agonizingly, Jesus took his last breath, to the horror of his mother and so many others around them. The broken and beaten body of Jesus now breathed its very last breath. It was finished.

The women who followed Jesus went into deep mourning, while the enemies of Jesus, who mocked him, beat him, then killed his body through one of the most torturous forms of public execution in history, rejoiced over their victory. Each follower of Jesus now knew the truth – if they were connected to Jesus by the same leaders who just killed him, they would likely receive the same beatings, torture, and death Jesus just endured.

Pause for a moment and consider what this would look like for you if you lived at this point in history as a follower of Jesus. What emotions would run through you as you encounter him dying on the cross? Is there an overwhelming sense of grief and sadness? Are you questioning God as to how anything like this could ever be right, or how he could let something like this happen?

Those who loved Jesus were mourning, but there was also a new level of fear they were facing. The One who brought them peace, protection, and comfort was now gone, and their worlds were turned upside down. His enemies had attacked out of nowhere, with one of his closest friends leading the angry mob to abduct him from the Garden in the middle of the night. They all knew the chief priests and Pharisees could come for them at any moment. Everything was completely different. The safety and security they once thought they had had now been obliterated and left in the dust. Maybe they didn't even realize they should have feared for their own lives. The idea of losing Jesus was beyond something any of them could have been prepared for, and I'm quite sure everything else around them felt awfully small.

The darkness lasted about three hours and lifted shortly after the passing of Jesus. Darkness is referenced in a few other places in God's Word. Job talked about darkness several times, once as a darkness hovering over him, the other was in reference to his life after losing his crops, his animals, his respect, and the lives of his children. In Exodus, God instructs Moses to lift up his hand over the land and cast a darkness upon the entire land of Egypt, a "darkness to be felt" (Exodus 10:21).

Possibly one of the most foretelling passages is John 12:35, "So Jesus said to them, 'The light is among you for a little while longer. Walk while you have the light, lest darkness overtake you. The one who walks in the darkness does not know where he is going.'"

Jesus was preparing his disciples and encouraging them to embrace the waning moments of their time together. We also know the disciples would be facing confusion and desperation as Jesus went to the cross.

1 John 1:5 says, "This is the message we have heard from him and proclaim to you, that God is light, and in him is no darkness at all."

As Jesus was dying, a heavy darkness blanketed the land and the true light that was Jesus Christ was leaving this world.

"For at one time you were darkness, but now you are light in the Lord. Walk as children of light" (Ephesians 5:8).

The scriptures tell us that before we connected our lives permanently to Jesus, we lived in darkness.

"He has delivered us from the domain of darkness and transferred us to the kingdom of his beloved Son" (Colossians 1:13).

The darkness we lived in was simply a life without knowing Jesus, which is a life without any hope. Darkness, terror, and violence are all part of our broken world, and Jesus came not only to become a part of it, but to save *us* from it. Jesus said he was a light, and once we have a relationship with him, we are also a light. As great and powerful as the darkness may be, there is still hope in the One name, the name of Jesus. The disciples and all followers of Jesus were facing a darkness like they had never experienced before. They had so many questions and so much pain from what had happened that they couldn't see that everything he predicted was about to come true. Sometimes this happens in the darkness. Sometimes we forget how much God loves us when we feel lost in the dark.

Chapter 15

Standing on the Counter Culture Corner

"You call me out upon the waters,

The great unknown where feet may fail.

And there I find You in the mystery,

In oceans deep,

My faith will stand.

And I will call upon Your name,

And keep my eyes above the waves,

When oceans rise, my soul will rest in Your embrace,

For I am Yours and You are mine."

- Oceans by Hillsong United

"What is this idiot doing???" I yelled to no one in my car, sharply swerving to my right. Out of nowhere this little man in red basketball shorts and a dirty white t-shirt had feebly attempted to jaywalk a busy road adjacent to the Dayton Mall, and did it just as I was flying by in my car. I noticed a slight limp as he lurched back and wondered if he could move quick enough to get thru traffic without getting hit. Why can't he be like normal people and use the crosswalk? I turned back and his second attempt was better than his first attempt of jaywalking madness.

Starbucks. After experiencing a jaywalker with a death wish, Starbucks was just what I needed. My Venti Blonde Roast with cream and the yellow packets was epic as usual, and I ended up having a very restful afternoon sipping away while burning through the final pages of an Ed Dobson book. I was doing everything I could on a superficial level to get my spirits up. Wearing my favorite shirt, a pretty fresh haircut, and with a glorious cup of coffee by my side, yes, life had gotten really tough, but today wasn't so bad anymore. After about an hour, I chugged the last few gulps of java heaven and headed on my way.

As I pulled near the corner of routes 725 and 741, there he stood. Oh. It was him again. In those red shorts and dirty tee, the man now stood on the corner with a sign. I didn't read his sign. I guess it didn't matter. It could have said, "Free Kittens here" for all I cared. I didn't need to know why he was out here, I just knew I was going to have to go talk to him. The Holy Spirit was doing something in me, and no one wants to miss those moments when God starts leading you in interesting ways.

Writer Henry Blackaby taught me in his book *Experiencing God* about how God is always working and how our objective is to just be in the room when it starts to happen. He taught me I didn't need to worry about what I was supposed to do or how to do it, I just needed to be available and be ready. Maybe this was going to be one of those moments. I wasn't sure, but I knew to pull the car over now.

I turned in at the BP Station and parked by the vacuums about a hundred feet away from the little man. I didn't realize I'd left my sunglasses on until I got closer and quickly pulled them off so he could see my eyes. It's pretty important to see someone's eyes when you talk, and it would be especially important with whatever this conversation was going to be. I walked down the small grassy decline toward the road and the man in the red shorts turned and saw me closing in.

Crap! There was a ton of stopped traffic now and it felt like everyone was sitting in their cars and gawking at the six foot two inch guy in a black Ramones T and ripped up jeans about to talk to a small beggar at the corner. I gave the little man my biggest grin as I got close and prayed for the words I couldn't get right in my thoughts.

"Hey man. You ok?" I asked.

"Yes" he said very cautiously.

"Cool. I'm Thad, and I just stopped to find out what's going on. What's your name?"

"Clarence," he said looking just a bit uncomfortable.

"Cool. Clarence. What's going on, man? Why are you out here?"

Taking a second to gather his thoughts, he looked me right in the eyes and said, "I'm trying to get a job and I need some money to get a place. There's a distribution center for a big store around here hiring and I've got an interview. But it's kind of tough to get transportation and cleaned up when you don't have a place to live, so I was trying to figure some things out today."

His body drooped, and with sluggish words, he had sounded even more exhausted than he looked. The entire time he spoke he looked me right in the eye and I believed everything he was saying was true. Even though I was struggling, and aren't we all sometimes, I knew the Lord wanted to encourage me through Clarence.

"Clarence, I'm going to be right back, ok? I've just got to do something real quick. But I promise I'll be back in a little bit, ok?" I asked.

"Sure. Do whatever you gotta do," he said.

I was off. I half jogged to my car and jumped in. I didn't know where I was going, but I knew I needed to get Clarence some food. He looked pretty thin and tired, so I knew this was a good start. McDonalds! Where was a McDonald's? Right! On the other side of the mall, and traffic was backed up all the way there. My mind raced, and then I realized where I was and remembered a Subway sandwich shop right around the corner. Great!

I pulled into Subway, walked in and toward the guy behind the counter, who greeted me with the ever obligatory, "Welcome to Subway! What can I get you?

"Well, it's not for me. I don't know. What's your most popular sub?" I asked.

He told me what it was and I said, "Sounds great! Let's get that and toast it and put whatever seems most popular on it. I'm buying it for a guy I don't know, so I'll trust you with it." I said with a grin

I could have stressed out over buying the sandwich for someone of whom I didn't have a clue to his tastes, but I didn't. I just stood there as the guy selected the bread, the meats he told me about, and added the vegetables he seemed to think anyone would like. He removed it from the toaster and shook some random shakers of salt and oregano all over it until he seemed fairly satisfied. He still asked me questions throughout this process, but I encouraged him to go with what he thought would be best and he was very helpful. As he finished, I grabbed some chips and water and asked one more question I couldn't believe I uttered, "Hey, do you sell gift cards?

2013 had been a brutal year financially, and in a million other ways, and things were probably as bad as they'd ever been. I didn't have the money for anyone's dinner, including my own. In this moment, though, I was compelled to have to make the wrong financial decision and do what seemed like the right thing for a guy who just needed a break. It wasn't anything grand or noble, and maybe it was irresponsible, but it was right.

I jumped back into my car and paused. The words still weren't there. I didn't know what to say to this man. Maybe I just hand him the bag of food and split. I prayed and just sat there for a while. Finally, I drove back to my new friend, Clarence. It had taken me longer than I thought and there was a chance he could have left, but I was hoping he'd still be there. I broke a few rules of the road, but pulled up in one piece and there he was. I thanked God for his help in this moment and asked for a clue of what words to say. I never seem to know what to say going into these situations. I got out of my car and walked back to the very busy road where Clarence stood. Traffic, again, was at a standstill, and as I approached Clarence, people actually started rolling their windows down, which made the moment just so completely awkward. We could both sense eyes drilled in on us and I was wondering if we could hide somewhere. A man in his forties, just sitting at the light in his pricey looking red convertible, lowered his sunglasses, staring us down, as if we were a couple of aliens hanging out at his favorite corner. His look enhanced my feelings that I just didn't belong on this corner with a homeless beggar, but none of that mattered when I began to speak.

"Clarence!" I hollered with a big grin as I got close. "I grabbed us some food."

Clarence walked to me and we stood about fifteen feet off the road. I noticed behind him a younger guy in a black jeep actually leaning across the front seat of his car staring at me, trying to listen to every word apparently. Their eyes were just all over us as I handed Clarence his food.

"I hope this is ok, man. I didn't know what to get, so I told them to just make it good. There's chips and water in the bag. Clarence, how are you going to get to the job interview? What if I gave you a ride? Do you have a phone where you can call me? I could drive you."

"I can use a pay phone," he responded, still seeming a bit suspect of me.

"Okay," and as I handed him a small sheet of paper. "Here's my number. Man, I can be like your job taxi service and I can get you to interviews or whatever, as long as I'm not working. And if I am, I've got friends who can drive you. What about getting a place to stay or more food? Here's a Subway gift card, but it's not much."

Clarence stared at his food and the gift card, smiling thankfully as he said, "This is good. Thank you. I have to tell them I have transportation so if you say you can help me, then I'll tell them I do."

"You've got a ride with me anytime, Clarence. And I've got backup for you, too."

Clarence turned to look back at the traffic behind him and realized the spectacle we had become. He might have been kind of used to it, but maybe nobody ever gets used to it. Maybe I had made it much worse than usual. He didn't seem to like it one bit and I didn't like all the people staring at us, either. It felt like a million eyes on me and not a smile around. I wonder if someone used the word idiot now when they looked at me. I smirked remembering how I'd used the same word earlier in the day regarding Clarence and thanked God for His forgiveness and how He's teaching me about love.

Suddenly, the words and everything came to me. I saw the world through my new friend's eyes for just a moment, and in that instant, it all made sense. Confidently, I reached forward and hugged a freshly shocked Clarence. It seemed like the right thing to do. I don't know why, but I felt like I needed to hug him. Then I quickly turned him around to face the traffic and I pointed right at all the people in their cars staring at us and found the words.

"Do you see them all, Clarence? All of these people driving by gawking at you and me? Let me tell you their story. They're just like me and you, man. They are hurting and struggling and desperate and they probably just wish they could catch a break, man. And here's the real thing you've gotta know. God loves you, man. He loves you just as much as anybody who drove by today. Did you know Jesus values you every bit as much as He values the President? You are that important to a wonderful and Holy God. No one has ever been more important to God than you, Clarence. You see, I'm suffering, too, and this has been the hardest year of my life, but I know God loves me and somehow He keeps helping me when things are at their worst. Anyway, I just want you to know God passionately loves you and Jesus gave everything for you. Look, I'm late and I've gotta jet, but you've got my number and I'll be waiting for your call. I've got some resources, Clarence, and we can find you a home and some help, alright man?"

Clarence nodded as I backed away and looked me dead in the eye with sincerity and said, "Thank you."

"No worries, man. I'm glad to help. Call me, Clarence."

As I walked away, I felt a rush of peace fall over me. He did it again. God was strong in my utter weakness, and I realized the only beggar I saw on that corner was myself. I begged God for the words. I begged God for an idea on how to help this guy. I begged God for grace for my new friend Clarence. I begged God for Jesus to come back soon and rescue sinners like me. Yes, I was grateful for the words, but I walked away grateful for Clarence, and for a Holy God with unending love.

An awkwardness sifted its way through me as I drove off. From the moment I stood on that corner with Clarence, I felt the cultural separations between us, and apparently the drivers pulling up to the stoplight next to us were feeling the same way. I felt like they couldn't keep their eyes off of us, and truthfully, it made me extremely hot and uncomfortable. Why did they have to stare at us? From my perspective, the people in their cars next to us did nothing to hide their curiosity. I wanted to help Clarence and it was important to me to become a part of his life, even if only for a moment. I needed to serve him, otherwise there would be no peace in me, just questions of "What if ...?" As I stood alone with Clarence, it felt like cultural opposition around me. I shouldn't have been there, at least in the eyes of those drivers. I was one of them, wasn't I? It would have been okay to hang a few bucks out the window to him, but getting out and talking to him seemed to cross the line of what is normal and what isn't.

It's something I never noticed before this moment, but there is only one man who appears during those harrowing moments following the death of Jesus on the cross in each of the Gospels of Matthew, Mark, Luke and John. A thick curtain of darkness had dropped onto Jerusalem and the surrounding areas, wreaking havoc throughout the city. While others fled and hid, Joseph of Arimathea willingly risked his life and livelihood to care for the body of Jesus. In a moment when others' fear drove them away, he found his courage and stepped into the fray.

When I was a kid, they played that old black and white Superman TV show super early Saturday mornings before most kids would be awake. I jumped out of bed early, watching them every chance I got. Looking back, it feels like almost every episode had a couple of steam trains racing towards each other at top speed, with Superman flying as fast as he could to stop the carnage. The passions and purposes of Joseph of Arimathea's life were about to collide head first, just like those old steam trains Superman stopped. It's hard to imagine the tension in that moment in history surrounding a man who was a devout follower of Jesus and an elder of the church.

"And when evening had come, since it was the day of Preparation, that is, the day before the Sabbath, Joseph of Arimathea, a respected member of the council, who was also himself looking for the kingdom of God, took courage and went to Pilate and asked for the body of Jesus" (Mark 15:42-43).

Courage. How in the world did he find his courage in a trial of this nature? It's no stretch to state Joseph of Arimathea had everything to lose. The shifting tide within the population of Jerusalem had raced terrifyingly fast from hailing Jesus as their hero to damning him to be tortured and sentenced to his death upon a rugged cross. Within five days the crowds went from shouting his praises and singing Hosanna to the wretched screaming for his blood. Even though the culture has shifted in Jerusalem, it wasn't necessarily the case with the council of elders. Since Lazarus was resurrected from the dead by Jesus, they had been trying to find a way to kill Jesus. This "respected member of the council" stood entrenched in a moment when he could have easily slipped away and hid, or he could have become someone else. If there was ever a moment when Joseph's fears and faith would collide, it was that moment. We quickly see, though, that fear never stood a chance.

Luke 23:50-51 shares how Joseph stood against the other members of the council of elders and refused to give his consent to the false conviction of Jesus. John 19:38 doesn't shy away from the emotions Joseph was facing, as his fear of the Jews was fully known and on display. Still, Joseph loved Jesus and couldn't just leave him without properly caring for his body and preparing it for burial.

> After these things Joseph of Arimathea, who was a disciple of Jesus, but secretly for fear of the Jews, asked Pilate that he might take away the body of Jesus, and Pilate gave him permission. So he came and took away his body. Nicodemus also, who earlier had come to Jesus by night, came bringing a mixture of myrrh and aloes, about seventy-five pounds in weight. So

they took the body of Jesus and bound it in linen
cloths with the spices, as is the burial custom of
the Jews. Now in the place where he was
crucified there was a garden, and in the garden a
new tomb in which no one had yet been laid. So
because of the Jewish day of Preparation, since
the tomb was close at hand, they laid Jesus there
(John 19:38-42).

He wasn't alone.

God had big plans for Joseph of Arimathea, and he never
intended for him to endure this responsibility alone. In
fact, the Father chose the most unlikely partner for
Joseph, a Pharisee by the name of Nicodemus. In John
3:1-21, Nicodemus went to Jesus and asked direct
questions about the message of Salvation through
himself that Jesus was teaching. Nicodemus wanted to
understand more about the idea of being born again, and
Jesus wasted no words when he replied, "'You are
Israel's teacher,' said Jesus, 'and do you not understand
these things? Very truly I tell you, we speak of what we
know, and we testify to what we have seen, but still you
people do not accept our testimony'" (John 3:10-11
NIV).

Nicodemus and Joseph of Arimathea resisted their
culture, and specifically their positions within their
culture, to serve Jesus, even after his death. It's a
Pharisee and a member of the council of elders who
come together in the dead of night to ask for the body of
Jesus. Talk about the most unlikely duo! Together they
prepared his body for a proper burial and laid him in a
tomb Joseph had purchased. Fear may have been part of
their experience, but it didn't stop them from following
the heart of God and showing their love for Jesus after
his death on the cross.

I may have experienced some awkward moments and feelings of opposition on that street corner with Clarence, but there was never anything of substance to fear. There have been countless times in my life unjustified feelings have stolen a moment of obedience, yet, as we see with Joseph and Nicodemus, God is capable of some pretty amazing plans, including giving courage to a couple of the most unlikely men. They didn't allow their feelings, fears, or the opinions of others to dictate their actions. They stood resolute and willing to serve Jesus, even after his broken body breathed its last breath on the cross.

It's these moments, sometimes these horrible, confusing, and agonizing moments where we battle against our fears, even if it's just being afraid of what a bunch of folks stuck at a stoplight might think of you. It's like the moment when my friend, Pat, told his wife and his friends that they weren't retiring to Florida, but rather that he a had a mission right there, right where they lived. It's like when that girl walked down in front of the whole church and told me, the broken shell of a man I was, how much God loves me and asked if she could give me a hug. It's like when you have to do something God is leading you to do, and a lot folks won't agree with you, but you go forward because you love Jesus. It was with this purpose these unlikely men of faith, this Pharisee and elder, came together and risked everything just to honor Jesus in his death.

Except, he wasn't dead. At least not for long.

Chapter 16

When Eden is Broken

"Well it took the hand of God almighty

To part the waters of the sea

But it only took one little lie

To separate you and me

Oh, we are not as strong as we think we are."

- Rich Mullins, "We Are Not As Strong As We Think
We Are"

The elegant round, white frosted, made-from-scratch birthday cake, candles and all, was set neatly on the table before me. Aunt Linda had outdone herself, once again. It wasn't my birthday, but my dad's, and everyone drew a deep breath together as we were about to sing. The song "Happy Birthday" must have echoed off the walls and for the neighbors to hear as our extended family gathered for a long weekend in Centerburg, Ohio to celebrate my dad's fortieth birthday. Aunts, uncles, cousins, my sisters, Mom, Dad, and Grandma Riley all indulged ourselves in that moment together celebrating Dad. What happened next, however, went down in the annals of the Riley family history for generation upon generation to come.

It was October 15th, 1975, and I was three going on four. If there was any age of appreciation of birthday cake, it was at this age, where everything sweet and gooey was a home run to my senses. The smell wafted throughout their dining room, overtaking the singing in my mind. I can't tell you what was going on inside my head at that moment, but it doesn't take a genius to figure out what my motives were. It wasn't about being first to try the cake, it was about how fast I could get some of it in my mouth. Sure, this was my Dad's birthday, but it was about to be my moment, and there wasn't a thing any of them could do to stop me.

While my family bellowed through the final portions of "Happy Birthday", a giant grin overtook my face, a gleam of tenacity unveiled itself in my eyes, and with the force of a locomotive bearing down on the good guy tied up on the train tracks, I flung my face forward, directly into my Dad's much celebrated birthday cake. With icing oozing out of the sides of my cheeks, my teeth and tongue went to work gobbling up a face full of the vanilla frosted angel food cake.

As I lifted my head in sheer delight, covered in cake and that massive smile, I realized the singing had stopped. My seven year older sister scowled at my icing and cake plastered face, while my younger cousin licked his lips, covered in nothing but sheer and unadulterated envy. The adults were stuck somewhere between shock and hilarity, and quite fortunately for me they eventually chose the latter. Laughter enveloped the room, and before I could take a second shot at this and dive back in, the massacred cake was speedily moved away. My face was roughly covered in hard pressed napkins as Mom tried to remove cake from my eyes, nose, cheeks, hair, neck, and eyebrows. Mom's aggressive clean up annoyed me a good bit. When you're three years old, you end up in these situations a lot, when your parents have to fix your disasters and sometimes they just need the equivalent of a fire hose to get the job done. It didn't matter so much what they did to me, though. I was still eating cake and would be tasting it for the rest of the night. At some point in the middle of the mayhem I created, a flash went off. Someone captured the moment on their camera, and that picture circulated throughout my family for many years. I don't know where it is today, but wherever it is, I'm sure it's provided a jolly chuckle or two. It's not everyday you can destroy something so seemingly perfect and get away with it, but maybe thanks to being both three years old and kind of a cute kid, it all worked out in my favor.

A three year old diving face first into his dad's birthday cake isn't going to destroy much of anything, outside of maybe the appearance of the cake. No one was hurt, no trust was broken, and there were no wounds to heal. I didn't have to ask anyone for forgiveness because my entirely family knew I was just a wild, little kid and didn't realize I was doing anything wrong. My actions were very intentional, but there was a deep innocence involved in that moment, one that would save me from any potential punishments or consequences within my relationships. My folks would trust me just as much as they did before, which wasn't a whole lot since I was three. This is what three year olds do, and everyone understands that they're pretty unpredictable and too young to know any better than to act on emotions and impulse. It's not, however, what twenty year olds do.

It was June 16th, 1992, and she was the girl who smiled. We were part way through our third week on Project in Virginia Beach, and the fifty-nine other students and I were having the summer of our lives! I'd been introduced to most of the other college guys and girls, but I'd never met this girl. She and her friend, Maria, were sitting at one of the twenty picnic tables shoved into the courtyard for us to eat dinner together at every night. Being the extrovert and very single college guy I was, it took about three seconds to make up my mind and start walking towards their table. I'd spoken with Maria a few times, but hadn't breathed a word to whoever this friend of hers was. Maria and her friend both worked with me at McDonalds, but I was on the grill and she was a cashier, so our worlds had no reason to collide.

"Hi," I said as casually as I could. "My name is Thad, and you and I are going to fall in love, and then I'm going to do something pretty horrible." At least, that's how the introduction should have started.

Sometimes it's a huge blessing God doesn't reveal to us how things are going to finally work out and what kind of pain we might cause each other. There were several fun and romantic moments we would share on that project together, and the first time we met was nothing but pure Bobby Brady fireworks for me. This is probably a little more accurate portrayal of that first interaction.

"Hi, my name is Thad. How's your evening so far?" I said with a big grin on my face.

"I'm Melanie, and it's going pretty well," the girl with the big smile said.

Her smile threw me, and before I could get my heart to slow down, I was sitting down next to her at that picnic table with the purple table cloth and sharing our stories. She was gorgeous, with the most sparkling, ocean colored blue eyes anyone had ever gazed into, and boy, was I doing a bad job of not being obvious about that gazing. She seemed very calm and confident, while I was doing my best not to make a complete idiot out of myself. Somehow she seemed to be interested in me and just kept smiling the entire time we talked.

I went to bed that night dreaming about her ridiculously perfect smile. Just over a week later we went on our first date together, and right there, in my little green Subaru, I made my first big move on a girl *ever*! With the skill of a three year old slamming his face into someone else's birthday cake, I reached over and snatched Melanie's hand. "Snatched" is probably the best word because of the high level of intensity in which I grasped onto her hand. If either one of us was about to be dangling off a ledge over a molten lava pit, that grip would have saved us. There was no doubt about it.

Our last night together on project, August 14th, 1992, I finally made my biggest move of all big moves and went in for my first kiss. Like, ever. It was beyond Bobby Brady fireworks, and I finally realized for the first time in my life why all this love stuff was so cool. She was heading home, though, to a place twelve hours and thirty-eight minutes away by mint, green Subaru. The memories of this moment at the beach, the long walks at sunrise next to the ocean, and a wild summer romance would have to be enough to hold us together, at least for the next three months.

Melanie was The Spin Doctors, and I was U2. She was Hartford High School's 1990 valedictorian. At Dayton Christian High School's 1990 graduation, while walking off of the stage, I opened my diploma when my friend shouted, "Thad! Is it signed?" Turning my head sharply to face the students sitting behind me, my hand lifted my diploma high in the air, flipped it opened and gave them and the entire crowd the biggest thumbs up possible. She lived in her world, a world where she gritted her teeth, dug her heels in, and clawed harder than anyone else through the mud of life. In my world, I was a lazy boy drinking diet root beer and watching action movies with my twenty best friends. She listened first and then spoke, while I never met a word I didn't like. I stood below her window jumping in puddles in the rain, while she watched me from above, smiling down on her clown.

Right before Thanksgiving, I boarded a midnight train out of Toledo, Ohio with what sounded like about fifty crying children. Melanie and I had been away from each other long enough, and it was time for one of us to do something. Since she was in college and I was working low paying jobs, I was the obvious candidate to journey across the country and start a new life with her. For the next twenty-seven hours, I took a train and a bus until I finally reached my new home in Hartford, Vermont. I was moving in with Melanie's parents and was going to try to find a way to make some money to eventually get my own place. My arrival felt like a bizarre celebration of sorts, filled with some worry and lots of hope. No one knew how I would find work and make it as a twenty year old college dropout living in a town that didn't have a whole lot of work to begin with.

For all of my insecurities, lack of focus, and selfishness, Melanie loved me with all of her heart. She was the girl of my dreams and everything I had hoped for in a life partner. We talked about our future together, including marriage and even having a family together.

My words, however, didn't match my actions. I'd come up with all kinds of lame excuses about not finding permanent work. Over the next few months, having her a few hours away at the University of New Hampshire made me more and more depressed. Melanie had worked hard to become her high school's valedictorian, and now she was a high achieving coed studying finance for her future in the business world. I was very alone in a small, quiet town, and she was on a campus filled with better looking, smarter, and richer guys than I could hope to be. The more depressed and helpless I felt, the more fear took over my worldview and my view of our relationship. In my weak and feeble mind, it was only a matter of time until she found a better boyfriend and moved on. If she wasn't done with me already, she would be soon, so I did the most pathetic thing I possibly could do to her. I got in my car and drove back to the Midwest and moved home. Without ever saying a word.

The painful words echo from the pages of her journal, written two days after I left, on February 13th, 1993 –

> Hi God. I'm hurting. Thad left for Ohio this Thursday. I guess we're over... I'm having a hard time remembering the good about Thad. But I knew he was generally very happy. He moved everything out of the room except the little things that had to do with me. Verses, pictures, turtles, letters... What's he thinking? Does he care? He must. It's all so weird. No goodbye. Maybe that was best. God, I know you have someone for me. I thought it was Thad. I haven't let go. I can't wait 'til he calls. I still think he's the one.

It was over. My first love, the first girl I ever kissed, all of it. It was simply over and, after the way I left, I knew there would be no going back and winning Melanie's heart. Over a month after I left, I finally called her and she received some cheap, token goodbye, not worth the $4.26 long distance bill it cost my parents. Whatever love and trust had once existed between us, I took a sledgehammer to it and bashed it ruthlessly. It was over.

In the history of mankind, that wasn't the first time trust was broken. It wasn't the first time someone made a really stupid choice and caused a major break, a seemingly irreparable break within a relationship. We see this in our world today, don't we? Politicians have lied to us and we struggle to trust our very own government. Hollywood stars commit adultery on their spouses, and suddenly there's another celebrity scandal and divorce. Your favorite athlete ditches your team and signs a big contract to go play somewhere else, and suddenly he's the last person you'd ever be caught cheering for. These breaks in relationship aren't something new to our world, and they've been happening for thousands upon thousands of years, actually.

In the scriptures, we see it as a common thread in the story of mankind's relationship with God. For instance, in the gospels we see Peter deny that he had any kind of relationship with Jesus. Throughout the Old Testament we see the failures of God's servants, such as David who committed adultery, Moses who killed a man out of a deep rage, Abraham who lied multiple times about Sarah being his wife, and King Solomon who disobeyed God's plans for him and pursued false gods. From Genesis to Revelation, the scriptures are chock full of the stories of men and women who struggled greatly in our world.

Every story has a beginning, and so does the story of how mankind broke their relationship with God. God did a pretty amazing thing when he created our world and us, and initially it wasn't a broken relationship. After God created man, he built a special place, the Garden of Eden, for man to live out his days. In Genesis 2, God brings Adam, the first man, into Eden and tells him, "You are free to eat from any tree in the garden; but you must not eat from the tree of the knowledge of good and evil, for when you eat from it you will certainly die" (Genesis 2:16-17 NIV).

Soon after, God goes way above and beyond for Adam and creates for him "a helper suitable for him" (Genesis 2:18 NIV). Adam fell into a deep sleep, and from one of his ribs God created Eve, and God has greatly blessed Adam, yet again. Adam and Eve spent their days in the Garden of Eden with all types of birds, beasts, and nature's beauty, and together they rule over the world God has created. This world, this perfect world with an overabundance of color, creativity, and beauty sits in the hands of a loving God who had given all of this to Adam and Eve for their pleasure and his purposes.

But there was that tree, that soon-to-be infamous tree with the special name and expectations. That tree was just sitting there directly in front of them in the garden. In God's perfect design for Adam and Eve, he had left them with unlimited resources, but even more than that, he had come to them with a great love. Somehow, through his brilliance and creativity, he had designed them with the ability to make choices in their lives. God withheld the notion that man should be simply created to serve him, but had decided it would be better for mankind to have a choice in the matter of how they will live their lives.

This unwarranted, undeserved, and irrational favor we call grace. Grace is like this massive box, wrapped beautifully, and tied with a perfect bow that we can only accept because of God's love for us. By his own perfectly loving nature, God bestowed upon Adam and Eve the profound gift of choice. We see it early in the story as Adam chooses names for the animals, and when Adam and Eve are not overpowered by God's presence in the garden. In fact, it was in a single moment when Eve was alone that the devil came in the form of serpent.

Now the serpent was more crafty than any other beast of the field that the Lord God had made. He said to the woman, "Did God actually say, 'You shall not eat of any tree in the garden'?" And the woman said to the serpent, "We may eat of the fruit of the trees in the garden, but God said, 'You shall not eat of the fruit of the tree that is in the midst of the garden, neither shall you touch it, lest you shall die.'" But the serpent said to the woman, "You will not surely die. For God knows that when you eat of it your eyes will be opened, and you will be like God, knowing good and evil." So when the woman saw that the tree was good for food, and that it was a delight to the eyes, and that the tree was to be desired to make one wise, she took of its fruit and ate, and she also gave some to her husband who was with her, and he ate. Then the eyes of both were opened, and they knew that they were naked. And they sewed fig leaves together and made themselves loincloths.

And they heard the sound of the Lord God walking in the garden in the cool of the day, and the man and his wife hid themselves from the presence of the Lord God among the trees of the garden. But the Lord called to the man and said to him, "Where are you?" And (Adam) said, "I heard the sound of you in the garden, and I was afraid, because I was naked, and I hid myself." (God) said, "Who told you that you were naked? Have you eaten of the tree of which I commanded you not to eat?" The man said, "The woman whom you gave to be with me, she gave me fruit of the tree, and I ate." Then the Lord God said to the woman, "What is this that you have done?" (Genesis 3:1-13).

It had once all been Eden, the perfect dwelling of man, God, and all of creation. Adam and Eve were the masters of their paradise and had everything they could ever want. Yet there came this one moment, a moment when the hearts of Adam and Eve wanted more than the utopia God had blessed them with. God may have given them a home and a purpose in paradise, but all it took was one fast conversation with the devil to steer them wildly off course. Satan had planted this idea, just one small idea in their head, the thought that they could be like God. Very willingly, Eve ate of the fruit, as did Adam, and they both chose to rebel against God, the same God who actually spent time with them in the garden. Even though they heard God's actual voice, walked with him in the garden, and were among his very first creations, none of it was enough for mankind. Adam and Eve made a choice to sin against God, not unlike the choices we make today. Our sin, our personal rebellions of the moment against God, have done the same thing. This sin caused a gap between us and God, and God wasn't about to leave us alone to die.

Jesus. This moment of sin, and every moment of sin for all of our existence, was redeemed by Jesus. God sent Jesus to us to create the bridge in the gap between us and God. The devil intended to permanently destroy mankind's relationship with God. Isn't that why he came to Eve in such a cunning and planned way? Satan's plans, once again, were completely and utterly annihilated because God already knew all of this was going to happen, and the plans for the redemptive and loving Jesus were in the works long before the serpent ever moved in the garden.

Jesus had to come to restore our relationship, and to this day he remains not only our greatest example of redemption, but, if we are willing to let him, he can be our very personal savior. Jesus came to do the will of His Father, and that will was to create an amazing path directly to him. The restoration of mankind could only be created by a perfect, omniscient, and holy God, and he gave us the greatest gift in Jesus anyone could ever receive. It is a complete gift, and by allowing your heart to be captured by God in this story of personal repentance and redemption through Jesus, it becomes your story, too. God gave us a chance to fix what we had broken and gave us a gift we can never repay. This is why Jesus came and this is an inkling of how much God loves you. We call the story of Jesus "The Good News", and rightly so.

God's plan was to take action to recreate a new relationship with him. He was never the one to cause the great divide between us and Him, that was our choice. Because of our choices to sin, God had to created a new scenario, one where the ultimate hero saves the world from itself. A scenario where the Son of the Most High God, Jesus, is born into this world. God knew, despite all that we had done and will do against him, he still wanted to forgive us and make this relationship work. He still loved us.

It was twenty-two years later on a brisk Ohio evening, and I was absolutely exhausted. Coming out of the darkest days of my divorce, there was an awkwardness about me, and I was finding much contentment in my moments alone. Dreams of one day moving to the Florida Keys, buying a fishing boat, and living out my days on the edge of the open sea were all I could hope for anymore. Maybe I'd be a short order cook working part-time, or just sit in a café alone while an overworked, pretty waitress served me endless cups of coffee as I poured out my heart in my latest book. Something strange on that night, though, stirred inside of me, and out of nowhere I started writing probably the most impulsive message I ever wrote. Before I could reconsider, I hit send, and as soon as I did I wished I could take it back, but I couldn't. It started off with two words, and those two words alone frightened me more than any start of any message I could remember.

"Hi Melanie."

Chapter 17

From The Coffee Shop

*"The door of God's mercy is thrown wide open,
and Christ stands in the door and says to sinners
'Come'."*

- Jonathan Edwards

It's 8:56 a.m. on Tuesday, March 21, 2017, and my chocolate raspberry coffee, lavishly resting inside its orange mug with a green and yellow stripe, is nothing short of perfection. Graham, the young man behind the counter, told me it's the last batch they'll carry and that they're on to the new maple walnut coffee at the end of this final pot. I'm not sure who makes these decisions, but I don't think filling out a comment card will be helpful. And does anyone actually use comment cards anymore, anyway? I'm not worried about liking the new flavor because French vanilla is an almost daily staple around here. Still, maple walnut sounds more like drinking a tree than coffee, but maybe I'm not the coffee guy I believe I am.

There's a young lady in a green shirt standing next to her table on the other side of the coffee shop and she just took the biggest bite of a sandwich I've ever seen someone her size take. A minute later, she's still chewing, and she might be for quite a bit longer still. I don't take the time to people watch so much around here because people watching and productivity are not good bedfellows. You and I could get caught up for a while wondering why the lady in the green shirt refuses to use a napkin, but my best guess now is that she wants to relive every morsel by licking her fingers clean of all the remains of that gigantic bite she just took. As you're reading this, she may actually still be chewing.

This is life in the year 2017, and can I be really honest and say I sometimes have to pinch myself that it is so good? The overabundance of blessings in my life are often too much for me to take in. I am a writer. I sit in a coffee shop two to three days a week and do this writing thing that I believe God wants me to do. This is how I follow Jesus. It's the best way I can walk down the path he has put in front of me. It's how I connect with the love of God and how I can best love his people. It was years ago, actually, that God first showed me my specific purpose, and he did it in the most overwhelming way.

I'm going to get really weird here for a few minutes, if that's okay. I'm going to take you back with me to the year 1999, to the Small Group Leader Retreat with Willow Creek Community Church being held in Milwaukee, Wisconsin. There were so many encouraging and challenging moments from the speakers and their messages, but it was in a quiet moment, in a reflective time of prayer, God took me somewhere I'd never been before and maybe I'll never go to again. At least in this life.

As I prayed, there was this vision which seemed to come to me. No, I didn't feel anything different, and I knew it was more in my brain than outside of it, but it seemed very real. I can't quite explain it, but maybe we could just agree to say it was a moment etched into the most real and vivid parts of my imagination. Okay, I'll stop making excuses and waffling around this, and tell you what I saw.

In my mind, I was flying into the clouds. Suddenly, I slowed down as my head poked through a cloud, followed by a slow ascension onto it. There on the cloud stood a figure, and I knew instantly who he was. Jesus! He wasn't like the stereotypes really, but he did have long, wavy, brown hair. He was very much Him, a being who was unique and unlike anyone I'd ever seen.

I was going crazy with excitement. Jesus! It was him! I grabbed him quick as lightening and hugged him as tight as I could. There was this unexplainable joy bursting from me, like nothing I could remember before. As I pulled myself away, I had a million questions and no clue how much time we would be together.

"Jesus!" I said with a massive grin.

"Yes, my son," he replied, with a strong and powerful, yet comforting voice

"What do you want me to do?" I asked, not even really knowing the question I was asking and what it pertained to. Was it right now? Or with my life? I had no clue until he answered me.

"Serve me with your life," he said, again in that same powerful, yet comforting way.

"How?"

"Love my people."

And as soon as the flying, the clouds, and Jesus came to me in this vision, daydream, or figment of my imagination, he was gone and I was back. It was over, but I sat there quiet and stunned. I remember feeling awkward all over and uncertain of what just happened. Maybe it was nothing. Maybe it was something, though.

Nothing within this vision disagreed with scripture, so maybe it had a little teeth. Maybe God wanted me to share this moment with him briefly, for just a moment in time, knowing the great trial that lay ahead well over a decade later. God knew there would be a shocking twist at the end of the this trial, that my children, reputation, and first love would all be restored to me. Maybe the purpose of this moment with Jesus wouldn't be found for another seventeen years when I started writing this book about Jesus and his love for us.

"Hi Melanie."

On December 10, 2014, Melanie Jean, the girl I first kissed in the summer of 1992 on the shores of Virginia Beach, exactly twenty-two years, three months, and twenty-six days earlier, walked down the aisle and became my wife. After over two decades apart, we found each other once more. For all those times when I prayed, when I begged God to bring back the love of my life, he was listening. I don't know why or how this all happened, frankly, and maybe that's okay. Maybe I don't have to understand what really made me drive away from her house in Vermont back to Ohio in 1993. How I reconcile all the tragedies and trials in this world isn't really important anymore, is it? I never dreamed when I sent her a message just saying hi that we would end up falling in love again and get married, but we did. After such a series of tragic and brutal losses, the Lord resurrected my life in Brentwood, New Hampshire, of all places. Just two years earlier I was living with my mom, dead broke, unable to be within five hundred feet of my home or even speak to my children. Today, my kids and I call New Hampshire our home and we can barely keep up with the blessings in our lives. After a few decades of sixty hour work weeks as well as working almost every weekend to make ends meet, I now passionately pursue this thing we might call a gift, this whole writing adventure.

I call her my most trusted friend, and she most certainly is. Melanie and I have created a new life together, a life built by two best friends who love Jesus, each other, and our six kids. Believe me when I tell you I totally am grateful for the blessing she has been to me in just a few short years, and I'm so much looking forward to spending the rest of our lives together. We both cannot wait for the new adventures that lie ahead! It has been a completely resurrected life for me in so many ways.

If 2013 was the year of deep hurt and confusion, than 2015 and forward have been the years of peace, healing and joy. But even within this new thrill, I've discovered in my relationship with Melanie that it all pales in comparison to what happened to Peter, John, Mary Magdalene, and Mary the Mother of James on a quiet Sunday in Jerusalem. Nothing in this world could compare to what happened inside of that tomb in Jerusalem.

It's tough to come up with the appropriate words that will take us into the story of the tomb where Jesus was laid. From all appearances, the devil had taken a baseball bat to the followers of Jesus, destroying all of their hope in just a couple of days. Imagine going from a deep fellowship with Jesus at the Last Supper to just hours later watching him being dragged off by an angry mob. The same Jesus who fed five thousand hungry followers was bloodied and beaten, carrying a cross through the streets of Jerusalem, and everyone knew what happened when a cross reached Mount Calvary. Remember the beatitudes? I bet the disciples and the rest of his followers did. Remember these words?

And he opened his mouth and taught them, saying:

"Blessed are the poor in spirit, for theirs is the kingdom of heaven.

"Blessed are those who mourn, for they shall be comforted.

"Blessed are the meek, for they shall inherit the earth.

"Blessed are those who hunger and thirst for righteousness, for they shall be satisfied.

"Blessed are the merciful, for they shall receive mercy.

"Blessed are the pure in heart, for they shall see God.

"Blessed are the peacemakers, for they shall be called sons of God.

"Blessed are those who are persecuted for righteousness' sake, for theirs is the kingdom of heaven.

"Blessed are you when others revile you and persecute you and utter all kinds of evil against you falsely on my account. Rejoice and be glad, for your reward is great in heaven, for so they persecuted the prophets who were before you"(Matthew 5:2-12).

This was the launching point for the Sermon on the Mount. Jesus had a crowd of people gathered around him and these were the words he preached to the assemblage who were hungry to hear him speak. It was words like these that confused and bothered the religious leaders of his day as Jesus catered to the impoverished and destitute again and again and again. The humbled, sick, weak, and lonely found a strength and a center of hope in the words Jesus spoke, but even more, in who Jesus was and what he represented. His followers loved him with every fiber of their beings and they knew they were greatly loved by him. They believed the hundreds of prophecies had been fulfilled and left everything behind to follow Jesus, the Son of God, the Promised Messiah. But in that one shocking and horrific moment in the Garden of Gethsemane, everything changed and before they could catch their breath, Jesus was left on a cross to suffer and die. He breathed his final breath while forgiving those who killed him. Darkness fell hard upon the land, echoing the loss of hope and the new despair found in those who still loved him, some staying at the foot of the cross until he was removed. After the darkness lifted, he was laid in the tomb and had been there for three days. Until…

And this wasn't going to be like Lazarus. Remember him? Jesus showed up at the tomb and commanded Lazarus to come out. In front of friends, families, and even some Pharisees, Lazarus was risen from the dead. He got up and walked out to the one who held power over death, Jesus. And if you remember, it was because of this resurrection the Pharisees knew who Jesus truly was, and they weren't about to bow down to a carpenter. Their plans had been executed, and in front of hundreds, maybe even thousands, Jesus Christ died on a cross. The Pharisees believed it was finally over, but they were wrong. Dead wrong. We go to the Gospel of John to experience the defining moment in our story, the resurrection of God's only son.

> Now on the first day of the week Mary
> Magdalene came to the tomb early, while it was

still dark, and saw that the stone had been taken away from the tomb. So she ran and went to Simon Peter and the other disciple, the one whom Jesus loved, and said to them, "They have taken the Lord out of the tomb, and we do not know where they have laid him." So Peter went out with the other disciple, and they were going toward the tomb. Both of them were running together, but the other disciple outran Peter and reached the tomb first. And stooping to look in, he saw the linen cloths lying there, but he did not go in. Then Simon Peter came, following him, and went into the tomb. He saw the linen cloths lying there, and the face cloth, which had been on Jesus' head, not lying with the linen cloths but folded up in a place by itself. Then the other disciple, who had reached the tomb first, also went in, and he saw and believed; for as yet they did not understand the Scripture, that he must rise from the dead. Then the disciples went back to their homes.

But Mary stood weeping outside the tomb, and as she wept she stooped to look into the tomb. And she saw two angels in white, sitting where the body of Jesus had lain, one at the head and one at the feet. They said to her, "Woman, why are you weeping?" She said to them, "They have taken away my Lord, and I do not know where they have laid him." Having said this, she turned around and saw Jesus standing, but she did not know that it was Jesus. Jesus said to her, "Woman, why are you weeping? Whom are you seeking?" Supposing him to be the gardener, she said to him, "Sir, if you have carried him away, tell me where you have laid him, and I will take him away."

Jesus said to her, "Mary."

She turned and said to him in Aramaic, "Rabboni!" (which means Teacher). Jesus said to her, "Do not cling to me, for I have not yet ascended to the Father; but go to my brothers and say to them, 'I am ascending to my Father and your Father, to my God and your God.'" Mary Magdalene went and announced to the disciples, "I have seen the Lord"—and that he had said these things to her (John 20:1-18).

Thirty-three years earlier, God the Father had sent his angels to proclaim the birth of his son. Once again, angels in white have came in the historic moment when God's Son once again breathed new life. Jesus was alive, and Mary of Magdalene was the first of his followers who saw him. In her grief mixed with confusion, she didn't even recognize the one who stood before her. She last saw him beaten, broken, and dying on the cross, but now she stood with him face-to-face. Maybe I'm being a bit hard on Mary Magdalene, but it's a little hard to understand how she didn't recognize Jesus. Maybe it was because of the images of what she had just witnessed, like the sight of the soldier piercing Jesus' side as water flowed out, indicating his death. Maybe she was wallowing in such grief she could barely lift her head and look him in the eyes. After his resurrection, his appearance might have slightly changed, just enough to cause Mary not to figure out that she should be exploding in joy! When Jesus said her name, however, she saw him for who he was.

This has been the toughest chapter for me to write. Can I share why? Let's start with the fact that it's nearly impossible to reconcile the powerful moment of Jesus' resurrection. As we read in the Gospels, the disciples came running to the tomb at break neck speeds! Mary

Magdalene couldn't recognize Jesus, and there were angels sitting in an empty tomb where Jesus was supposed to be. God had sent his son, his sinless and perfect Son, to be sacrificed so all men who come to Jesus might be saved. This in itself is the most essential moment in the history of all of mankind. Satan thought he was all set, but the twist was that he was doing God's bidding the whole time. Now the great advocate of man stands before God the Father as a perfect sacrifice and the Great Judge looks upon those who love, know, and obey Jesus and only sees our Savior. He sees Jesus. And who was it...seriously here...who was it to first see Jesus upon his resurrection? Was it the Roman Emperor? Was it King Herod? Maybe even the religious leaders? No, it was a woman who was once possessed by demons, who sat faithfully alone outside of his tomb mourning his death. Just Mary.

Or maybe it was just you.

Can I ask you a few questions? How are you doing right now? Are you grieving something? Do you feel hopeless or in despair? Maybe you don't right now, but do you remember maybe the last time you did? I bet it's not so hard to wrap your head around. You have been there, too, I'd bet. I'd wager you've had a moment or four in your life when you felt completely hopeless and saw your world come crashing down all around you. Is it so hard to relate to Mary Magdalene in her mourning and heartache? I think not. In fact, I bet you can relate perfectly.

You see, you are Mary Magdalene in her grief. You are John looking on at the carnage of the cross in despair, wondering how any of this could be good. I bet you're also Peter denying God in your life when you should have been taking a stand, not the easy way out. There may have been moments when you felt like Judas or have experienced a moment of deep betrayal in your life. The followers of Jesus we read about in the Bible faced grief, failure, betrayal, struggles with money, and overwhelming feeling of loss and discouragement. They lived in a constant state of intimidation within their culture and faced opposition when all they were trying to do was help people understand how much God loved them. The more they followed Jesus, the more challenged they were. This life of being a follower of Jesus has never been something the world embraced as truth, but more often than not we are viewed as being religious. By religious, I mean we categorize Jesus into a certain section of our lives instead of centering him as the purpose of our entire existence. In America today, living a good life is the culturally accepted credo and motto. Being religious is considered just a piece of this pie, not the entire pie itself. Imagine being Mary Magdalene, consumed by grief, and suddenly realizing that you are standing with Jesus and he is alive!

The moment Mary realized Jesus was alive, her entire world was changed forever, and so was yours. No one has ever seen anything like this incredible moment before, have they? Well not exactly, but we do see similarities throughout scripture, like when Esther risked everything and the king not only believed her, but he destroyed her people's enemies.

It's like when Israel (formerly known as Jacob) first saw that his beloved son, Joseph, was alive after years of believing that he had been killed.

It's a little like Noah when the dove came back to the boat with the branch in its mouth.

It's like that moment when the king yelled for Daniel, who'd been in the lion's den all night, and Daniel yelled back, "My God sent his angel and shut the lion's mouths, and they have not harmed me!" (Daniel 6:22).

It's like when Elijah stood toe-to-toe with 450 prophets of Baal and God suddenly sent fire down from heaven, consuming the water soaked altar Elijah created.

It's like when the angel stopped Abraham's knife from striking his only son and God provided a ram for the sacrifice.

It's like when manna fell from heaven on the Israelites, despite their bitterness toward Moses and God.

Or like when the widow's jar of oil refused to be empty.

And like the moment Goliath went down and David rose up.

It's like when Shadrach, Meshach, and Abednego stood in the fiery furnace, but the king saw there was a fourth.

Or like how Moses parted the Red Sea to save all the Hebrews from the Egyptians.

And like when Shamgar struck down six hundred Philistines with an ox goad. You should look up ox goad, because when I did it made me feel smarter.

It's like knowing this woman across the coffee shop taking giant bites of food is known and loved by God, just like you and me, and that God knows everything about her and loves her just the same, giant bites and all.

It's like when I sat in that McDonald's parking lot in Wayne, Ohio, sobbing my eyes out, asking God to bring back the love of my life, and less than two years later I'm married to the first girl I ever kissed and who I hadn't seen in over twenty years.

It's more than all of this, though, and so much more. Yes, the story of God's people throughout the scriptures are soaked in his rescue, restoration, and salvation. My story and the life I live today is a complete testament of God's love and blessings, as he has completely restored my life and made it even so much better than what it was just a few years ago when I was filled with such deep agony and exhaustion.

The story of the resurrection of Jesus, however, is unique because it is more than just the rebirth of a man. It is about hope being wrenched from the fires of hell and coming alive in the heart of every woman, man, and child throughout the entire earth. This isn't just Mary Magdalene's story, this is *my* story. And this is your story, if you choose.

Yet many, maybe even you, will choose for this not to be their story. Many choose a life of serving self or simply being unwilling to believe that they need to be rescued by Jesus. It's the saddest of all the stories, because that story ends in a terrible, horrible ending. There's no redemption. There's no eternity in paradise, no standing in the presence of everyone who loved God before you, but worst yet – there is no meeting God the Father, the Holy Spirit, and Jesus face-to-face. There is nothing but eternal suffering if you choose not to follow Jesus, and understanding that truth in itself is an amazing grace. That God would actually provide a clear and focused path to a relationship with him is beyond our wildest dreams and expectations. That God loves us so very much, each of us, that he would make a way to him, a bridge, so that we can reclaim the relationship that Adam and Eve lost long ago in the Garden of Eden is the base truth this entire story. To deny this path is to deny him your heart, and there is no relationship if you can't give someone your heart. I know that might sound a little weird, but this is what the bible teaches us.

"If you openly declare that Jesus is Lord and believe in your heart that God raised him from the dead, you will be saved. For it is by believing in your heart that you are made right with God, and it is by openly declaring your faith that you are saved" (Romans 10:9-10 NLT)

It's your heart captured by the grace, beauty, and love of Jesus, and then a confession of all these things to God and the world we live in today that will save you from eternal separation from God. This is what it means to know Jesus, and this is why God sent him to us. I know it isn't the way you and I would probably do things if we were God, but we can thank God also for that! God designed a perfect and unique way to him, not some path that's confusing and riddled with guilt, exhaustion, and pain. God simply sent Jesus, his son, to rescue the world and we basically get to saddle up our horses and go with him on this wild journey.

There is no other path, there is no other way to the Father. Jesus said, "I am the way, and the truth, and the life. No one comes to the Father except through me" (John 14:6). There's no ambiguity; zero need to be confused. There's no heavy lifting on your part because Jesus and the Father already did the heavy lifting. It's simply a choice.

So, what will you do? If you don't know Jesus, what will you do. You see, right now you are her. You are Mary Magdalene. Maybe for the first time ever you're seeing Jesus standing outside of the empty tomb and you have to decide what you are going to do. If you're like Mary, then the excitement booms up from your gut, through your throat, and you cry out for him. Or this moment of recognition will pass you by as something to smile and nod at, but for you, it doesn't really work like that.

Or maybe it does. What will you do?

Chapter 18

My Time Is Yours

"Let God have your life. He can do more with it than you can."

- Dwight L. Moody

> And (Jesus) said, "Yes, it was written long ago that the Messiah would suffer and die and rise from the dead on the third day. It was also written that this message would be proclaimed in the authority of his name to all the nations, beginning in Jerusalem: 'There is forgiveness of sins for all who repent.' You are witnesses of all these things" (Luke 24:46-48 NLT).

It feels almost impossible, doesn't it? It seems too intense to wrap my head around this idea while my low rise Converse Chuck Taylors take me with my dog, Trip, down Abbey Road in Brentwood, New Hampshire. How am I supposed to understand this truth as I look up at the stars shining bright in the night sky? Comprehending the idea that God, who created the spectacular night sky filled with those brilliant stars, is the same God who loves and knows me, including the worst of me. It feels like it is almost too much to consider. The God who created every mysterious creature in the deepest parts of the oceans is the same God who sent Jesus to Bethlehem to become our personal Savior. Couldn't God do so much better than to sacrifice his only Son for someone like me? If he knows me, how is this even possible? I don't deserve Jesus, but just because I don't deserve him doesn't mean I'm not sprinting to him at full speed with my arms open wide.

From the beginning in the Garden of Eden until the final moment when he returns, Jesus Christ is the most influential figure ever to grace our planet. I was four when I first began to understand who He was, yet others might be ninety-four when they embrace Jesus as their king for the first time. Age is of little relevance here. His story of love and sacrifice hasn't only changed my life, but it has profoundly impacted the whole world forever. What he did for us, and maybe more importantly *why* he did it for us, leads us into the most important decision each of us will ever face. There was no existence greater and more significant than the life of Jesus who, in his final days, defeated death and claimed all of our rottenness, ugliness, and sin for himself. That action was so much more than a sacrifice because what Jesus did was also about an amazing power to carry all of our sins upon himself in order to restore our relationship with God.

A few years ago I finished reading the last book in an adventure series. Honestly, it ended a bit flat, but how the hero destroyed the evil king was rather interesting. In the story, the protagonist used magic and went into the king's mind, walking him through every inch of the pain, violence and torment he had brought upon his people since the moments he had come to power. What was quite fascinating was that the good guy led the king through each scene from his victim's perspective. As these images stuck the villain, the bad king went insane, lost all of his power and was easily defeated. All it took to end the evil king's reign of destruction was to force him to endure in his mind the evil things he had done to others.

We, however, have the greatest of all kings, our King Jesus. An innocent and holy Jesus captured the sins of the world and brought all of them upon himself. Talk about something completely and utterly unbearable! I can't even begin to comprehend what it would look like for murder, rape, all sorts of fornications, hate, and violence to be thrown onto any one person, let alone someone so innocent. When we say Jesus had to "bear" our sins on the cross, it's a complete understatement. How he did this is not only amazing, but it's the most horrific thing anyone has ever had to endure.

He did this for everyone, regardless of who they are and what they have done. He has given every person the opportunity to have their sins forgiven and to create a new life with him. We saw this example first in his relationships with his disciples. He hadn't chosen these twelve men because of their education or even their own persistence in following the religious rules of the day. We have seen throughout the Gospels that those who loved the law didn't always love Jesus. We have also seen how Jesus has captured the hearts of so many unique people from every nationality, background, culture, age, and everything else you can imagine. God the Father created the plan, and Jesus came to us as our Savior, our Sacrifice, and our King.

Jesus is affecting lives today just as he did when he walked this earth. He tells us in John 14:12, "I tell you the truth, anyone who believes in me will do the same works I have done, and even greater works, because I am going to be with the Father." As Jesus walked this earth in a life dedicated to honoring his Father, so many others follow in his footsteps today. It's a little tough to wrap our heads around the idea that we could do things similar to Jesus, isn't it? How does this actually happen?

My friend, Kevin Spencer, has one of the most interesting ministries of encouragement I've ever encountered. Kevin is a runner, and when I say he's a runner, I mean this guy can run almost any race you'd put him in. Kevin loves a big challenge, and he's ready for just about anything you could throw at him. I met Kevin when I began attending Rainbow Forest Baptist Church in 2007 while living in Roanoke, Virginia. One morning I was leaving early for work and opened the front door to encounter a bit of a bizarre sight. For some strange reason, the windshield wipers on my 2001 Hyundai Elantra had been lifted up. It was a curious sight to see my wipers pointed straight up to the sky. Pausing just long enough to stare in wonder, I determined it must have been the silliness of some bored neighborhood kids. I laughed it off, put my wipers down, and drove to work. A few days later it happened again, and then again on Sunday morning, making that the third time it happened in one week. I was beginning to wonder if there was a more serious problem happening around me. I still laughed a little about it, but my laugh had less of a happy chuckle and more of a creepy feel.

That same Sunday morning, I walked into Rainbow Forest Baptist Church and saw Kevin Spencer dodging people to get to me. He wore this huge, silly grin, which really wasn't a remarkable thing for my friend. He greeted me and shook my hand saying, "How has your week been, Thad? Has anything strange been happening?"

I wasn't quite prepared for this greeting, and since he caught me off guard, I simply responded, "Um…I don't think so."

"Are you sure, Thad? There's nothing different in the morning when you leave the house?" he said, holding onto that grin.

All of a sudden I remembered and said, "Yes! Someone has been messing around with my windshield wipers and lifting them up!"

Kevin looked at me with satisfaction and said, "You know, when I am out on a run, I sometimes run by my friend's houses and pray for them. If they ever see their windshield wipers up, they can just know while I was out on a run, I was praying for them and their family."

It would be another year and a half before I became a runner myself, but Kevin helped me become an encouragement to others. Random friends of mine throughout the Miamisburg area would wake up to the wipers pointing to the heavens on their cars. Eventually I let them know what I had done and my reasons for doing it. Some of them had been a little concerned about what seemed like a targeted prank from the neighborhood kids, but once they knew I was praying for them, they looked forward to those mornings of raised wipers.

Kevin's gift of prayer extended from the love and joy that his relationship with God brought him. He understood not only the power of prayer, as Jesus did in the Garden, but he also passionately loved his church, like Jesus did when he washed the disciple's feet. Too often the church receives unfair criticism based on a few bad apples and the workmanship of our enemy, Satan. While some have chosen to become angry and bitter, there will always be people like my friend, Kevin, who just want to be a little bit more like Jesus, and love the people around him.

It doesn't take much sometimes. I think a lot of us look at the person preaching or someone with an incredible talent and say, "I could never do anything like what they can for God." Jesus was less concerned about the specifics gifts and always concerned about the heart of the individual serving him. We often see this battle today, more than ever, as technology and media have catapulted some Christian ministries and pastors to the forefront. Too often we can get overwhelmed with the idea that our gift doesn't mean as much, when in truth it means everything.

Jesus dug into the motives and heart of each person who claimed to love God and wanted to serve him. That is why he praised the poor widow we read about in chapter nine. It's why tax collectors, prostitutes, fishermen, shepherds, and men sentenced to death called him King, while he called them his brothers and sisters. The blind shouted boldly, lepers came and he touched them, children came freely, and even demons bowed before him. Jesus did something no one else was ever able to and no one has been able to do since. Jesus Christ came to us and created a perfect path between himself and the God of the Heavens. He took every single sin, every single bad thought, every single ugly word uttered, and everything else bad we ever could conceive and exchanged them for his perfect life. Then he died at the hands of men who just couldn't accept him, this humble man, as their Savior and the Savior of the world.

I don't know why I messaged them, but I did. After observing one of their posts on social media, I decided it was time for us to meet. It seemed like all the commenters were frustrated, and they seemed kind of frustrated, too. It was probably the worst time of my life to reach out to them, because nothing seemed to be going my way. Maybe God was leading me to do this? I took a chance and asked them to meet me for a beer and to have a conversation about God.

In 2013, my life had become so different for so many reasons, but probably nothing was more strange than me asking a couple of atheists to hang out with me. I wanted to meet with them because it was important to me to understand why they no longer believed in Jesus. It was also important for me to listen to their stories and to try to understand how anyone could not want to throw themselves head first into God's love and grace. I had gotten to know them recently because of their debates and outspokenness on social media, which had given me some ideas about their conversion. What they posted wasn't enough to help me understand, though. I needed to talk to them face to face.

I asked the hostess if my friends were there yet, and she let me look around. After a few moments I spotted them sitting on the front patio, and my heart sped up just a little. I had prayed about my time with them, not really knowing how this evening would end. We spent a lot of time listening to each other's stories. I was willing to share some of the darkest moments of my life, and you should have seen the looks on their faces. Good grief, they looked so surprised! Maybe they didn't expect me to be so honest, or maybe they just expected me to throw out Christian cliches the whole night. I wasn't interested in convincing them of anything, because we don't need to convince people about Jesus and his love for us. They are either captured by the magnificent splendor of it all, or they choose not to be. I attempted to be as honest as possible, especially about my trials and shortcomings, and allowed them to come at me with every idea, doubt, and argument they had. I didn't try to debate the whole night away. I just listened, mostly, and disagreed when it seemed appropriate.

At the end of the evening, one of them looked at me and said, "Maybe you actually do need God. Maybe you should keep your beliefs. Maybe you shouldn't change anything." The other nodded in complete agreement.

It was a surprising statement, and I think they were a little surprised by it, too. Both of them were in agreement, and it was more than I had hoped would happen. Neither of them were convinced that having a personal relationship with God was important, but they both agreed someone like me, someone who had fallen on hard and troubled times, needed to keep the one thing people who are suffering desperately need. Hope.

Driving away, I reflected and later wrote down my thoughts regarding our time together. Regardless of the topic, they always had a polished argument against my belief in God. They threw out tough Old Testament questions and truly were incredibly well versed in various theories of modern science and their apparent opposition to certain scriptures. I listened to every word they said, sometimes with an appropriate defense, but sometimes I stayed silent, and I was ok with not having so much to say. If there was ever any hope of either of my friends calling upon Jesus to become Lord of their lives, it was going to be found in the love of Jesus and what he did for them. They would have to cling to the words of Jesus, such as when he said, "Peace I leave with you; my peace I give to you. Not as the world gives do I give to you. Let not your hearts be troubled, neither let them be afraid" (John 14:27).

When we read the words of Jesus, it can stir in us incredible feelings of trust and love, knowing he is the one who can bring us an empowering relationship with God. Some are left with nothing but doubts and denials. Many hear words like this and are unchanged, unwilling to seek the truth of the love of God sent here to change our lives forever. I don't think I'll ever understand why anyone wouldn't want to be rescued from a tough and meaningless existence in this life. We have a chance to have an eternal purpose and to love the God of the universe and the people of this world.

One of the most difficult ideas to teach children is why we need to repent and ask for forgiveness when we've done something wrong. Somehow they know from an early age how difficult this is, most likely because of the purpose behind what they are doing. I have yet to see a child gravitate naturally towards repentance, and to do so enthusiastically, but if they do, it is very likely a learned thing from the parents. It is, however, one of the most urgent aspects of the Christian life. Without an understanding and acceptance of our personal need for repentance and forgiveness, we cannot have a relationship with God. There has to be a desire to go to God and move forward in his grace and love. This is the freedom Jesus brings to each of us, but there is no freedom without repentance and forgiveness.

Jesus came in a revolutionary manner at a revolutionary time. His coming was the beginning of freedom, the type of freedom no other religion or movement could offer. Identifying ourselves as sinners in need of Jesus isn't the easiest thing to do, but it is the path to the freedom Paul talks about when he says, "For freedom Christ has set us free; stand firm therefore, and do not submit again to a yoke of slavery" (Galatians 5:1).

It seems easy, doesn't it? It seems like choosing to embrace the seemingly reckless and radical love of Jesus is almost a foregone conclusion, but for so many it is not. God doesn't love us because of what we can bring to him or how we deliver for him in this relationship. It doesn't change or destroy God when we walk away from him and reject his love, but he keeps offering it to us every step of the way. In this life, God's love is always available to us, but some of us will be like the ones who listened to what Jesus said, yet refused to believe. Jesus said in Matthew 13:14-15, "'You will indeed hear but never understand, and you will indeed see but never perceive. For this people's heart has grown dull, and with their ears they can barely hear, and their eyes they have closed, lest they should see with their eyes and hear with their ears and understand with their heart and turn, and I would heal them.'"

It was August of 1992, and one of the last nights at the end of summer project in Virginia Beach with CRU. There had been great days, and there had been tough days. I had fallen in love with my future wife, made friendships for a lifetime, and experienced all of the highs and lows of engaging in such an adventure. Even working at McDonald's had been a great experience, though I didn't like having a chicken salad being thrown in my face.

"Is the chicken fresh in this salad?" she snarled at me. "It doesn't look fresh at all!"

"It is ma'am. In fact, I just caught it out back, killed it, cooked it, and placed it on here for you," I said with a smile.

I totally deserved to be scolded fiercely, but instead, the lady picked up the salad and threw it like a frisbee, hitting me right in the upper lip. It was a great throw, and she suddenly seemed quite satisfied. To add to my embarrassment of having salad hanging off my face, I was even more displeased when she pointed at me and said, "You shouldn't be talking like that!"

I felt humiliated and angry, shouting with a small quiver in my voice, "Well, you shouldn't be throwing chicken salads at people's faces!"

My manager instantly came up and gently moved between us, as she suddenly turned her venom towards him. He was very kind, and she eventually calmed down, and I felt like the biggest idiot, standing there wishing the dressing hadn't been previously poured on the salad. The lady finally took a new salad and headed over to her table, and I made my way back to the grill to cook up some more of those chickens I never actually killed with my bare hands. It was totally my fault, and I apologized humbly to my manager. Fortunately, he was very gracious and we shared a laugh about the whole situation.

Scottie was another manager who worked with us that summer. If there was ever a witty and fun manager to work with, it was my new friend, Scottie. He could take almost any situation, and there are certainly some interesting situations at McDonald's, and make you laugh. He had a great sense of humor. He was a year older than me, just twenty-one years old, and seemed to know everything about working at McDonald's. We quickly became friends and I began praying for him.

Throughout the summer, I learned a little more about Scottie's life, though he wasn't offering up a lot of information. It took a little bit of digging in between him shouting out that he needed "cheese on twelve" and all the other things you might hear working the grill at McDonald's. Everyone liked Scottie and he made working there about as much fun as you could have being twenty years old and working the grill at a crazy, busy, beach-front McDonalds. It wasn't the worst job ever, but I probably wasn't one of their better cooks. I guess not much has changed with my cooking over the years.

Every year at summer project, CRU hosts an employer dinner where they invited everyone we worked for during the summer. It was a *big* deal. At the dinner, one of us stood up to speak from each place of employment about some of our experiences of the summer and how much we appreciated working for our employers. I was chosen to speak from the McDonald's employees of the project, and frankly, I did a horrible job. I stood up and rambled on and on about how tough it was for me that summer. Basically, I just whined to about a hundred or so people. I don't know if I actually said anything worth listening to, and I am still embarrassed by this very public failure. One of my closest friends on project, a young man from Virginia named Sean Fitzgerald, had worked with me at McDonald's that summer and talked to me later that night by his bed in the guy's project house.

"That was tough tonight, bro," Sean said to me with a tint of compassion in his eyes.

My head had hung low since I walked off the stage, and it was obvious to me, too, what I had done.

"I'm sorry, man. I totally blew it for you all and am really, really sorry. I should have insisted you do it," I muttered, barely able to look my friend in the eye.

"It was bad, but it's okay, bro," said my friend, who used the word *bro* like he was paid every time he said it. "What truly matters is the way we worked for them this summer, not your words at the end. In that light, you did well."

"Yeah, but it doesn't change what I did tonight," I barely said above a whisper.

"Well, I forgive you and everyone else will, too. Why don't you just get some rest? Tomorrow is a new day, and you'll feel better in the morning. You're a good dude, Thad," Sean said with his million dollar smile.

"I think I need to go for a walk. Maybe I'll go down to the beach for awhile."

"Okay, but make sure you get some rest tonight, bro," my friend said as I nodded and turned to head out the door.

Stepping out onto the sidewalk I felt like a pathetic fool and asked God to forgive me for blowing this important moment for all of us. I had been entrusted with the opportunity to share the beauty, love, and purposes of God, but I ended up talking more about my own drama than about the hope and salvation through Jesus Christ. In my eyes, I had ruined what could have been such a special moment for the whole project, all of my fellow McDonald's employees, and our employers.

Just a few minutes later the sand of Virginia Beach was in between my toes one more time. Maybe I could clear my head a little by inhaling deeply the sights and smells of the Atlantic Ocean. As I took off my sandals, slightly burying my feet in the sand, I gazed mournfully out into the night time waves. Deep breath after deep breath brought me back just a little from a pretty tough place. It was the end of my summer here, and although it had been the adventure of a lifetime, I ended it looking like a selfish, immature jerk. This wasn't going to happen to me ever again, because tonight I learned to keep my mouth shut. If people wanted to hear me speak, they'd have to pry my mouth open, because nothing worthwhile would probably ever come out of my stupid mouth again. How could I have been so selfish to blow this opportunity and to embarrass myself in front of the entire summer project and our employers? All I wanted to do was go crawl under a big rock and hide from the rest of the world.

As I looked out to the never-ending incoming waves, there was a slight movement out of the corner of my eye and I turned to look. His head hung low as his feet trudged heavily through the sand. He must have recognized me from a distance. Barely glancing up, he was coming my way on this dark and lonely night. Every sluggish step seemed almost too heavy for his body, as if he were carrying the weight of the world on his shoulders. There was no doubt he needed a friend to listen, and then do the one thing I wasn't going to do anymore. Whatever he was doing here didn't need to involve me. If God was about to do something, right now wasn't the time and it didn't make any sense. I turned my eyes back to the ocean, knowing I wasn't up to the task, which I had more than proved publicly tonight. I had nothing to share and nothing to give. This couldn't be happening, not when these stupid tears are stuck in my eyes. Please, Lord, let him turn and head the other direction, but I could see him out of the corner of my eye. He was getting closer.

"No. No way. Not right now, God. I can't do this," I pleaded under my breath.

Regardless of my overwhelming feelings of humiliation from my epic failure, my manager Scottie was still taking those heavy steps in the sand until he finally came to a stop just a few feet to my left. I turned away from the comfort and safety of my wondrous view of the ocean and looked at him, taking a deep breath, then finally letting the air out of me slowly. The young man lifted his head to look right at me, exposing the tears that welled up in his eyes. There we both stood watching each wave get a little closer as it scurried across the sand. We were two very broken and wounded men, now facing each other on a beach late at night, waiting in silence until one of us finally found the courage to finally say something.

"Thad. You gotta minute?"

"Sure, man. My time is yours."

Chapter 19

For The Journey Ahead

*"As God more fully equips your ship to sail in
storms, he will send you on longer voyages to
more boisterous seas, so that you may honor him
and increase in holy confidence."*

- Charles Spurgeon

I turned a little away from Scottie to face the ocean now
crashing down in front of us and said, "It's a heck of a
night out here."

The waves ran up onto the beach as the water came
closer and closer to our feet. In my peripheral vision, I
saw him wipe those red eyes he no longer cared to hide.
Whatever brought a confident, young guy into such a
state was a mystery. God had put us both here together,
though, and I was going to see this through to the end. I
smirked a little to myself, considering my foolishness
earlier in the evening. If God wanted something to
happen, it was going to happen. Good grief, hadn't I at
least learned that by now? The breeze of salt air kept us
somehow isolated from the burdens we both held onto.

Exhaustion was etched deep into his face, but Scottie
didn't act like he wanted to be alone, which surprised me
a good bit. He was a confident young man who always
liked being the guy with all the answers. He wasn't
cocky, though, and you could sense a bit of humility in
him. All of this, however, was washed away in that

moment, because whatever was bothering Scottie was probably the only thing on his mind.

"It's a nice night out here," he replied. "I come out here to think sometimes."

"I come out here sometimes, too. Just to walk and think. I guess there's no better place to be on a night like this. But hey, are you okay, man?"

Scottie dipped his head and said, "No, it's been a really rough night. A lot of people are upset and I don't really know what to do."

It got real quiet real quick and neither of us said anything. I just looked at Scottie, intending to bear a kindness and openness on my face. He was acting like he wanted to talk, and after everything I had done earlier in the evening, I was more than ready to listen. Scottie looked up at me, maybe wondering why I hadn't said anything. We just stood there for a moment until he finally broke the silence.

"It's my family, Thad. There's a bunch of stuff happening. It sucks and I'm pretty upset about it all. There's kids involved, and they're crying and I don't know what to tell them or how to help. My whole family is pretty confused and torn apart, and we are all really close. I haven't been perfect, but who is? The whole thing is just horrible and I guess it's hitting me pretty hard tonight."

Scottie could barely hold back his tears, and suddenly it seemed far too many people were on this beach. Where did they all come from? I needed to get him out of here and someplace where we could really talk. It was no coincidence Scottie and I had found each other on this fateful evening, and now God was showing me it was time to leave my self loathing in the dust. Scottie looked uncomfortable, as over-my-shoulder he saw some friends from the project walking toward us, heading from the boardwalk out onto the beach. It was time for us to get moving before anyone else could delay the moment for either of us.

"Hey Scottie. Why don't you come back to the project house with me for a little while? I bet you'd like to see where we all stay and we can hang out there," I said. It was the only idea I could come up with in the moment.

"Uh, sure. Why not?" he replied, and we walked off towards the boardwalk. I smiled and acknowledged my friends quickly as we passed, and fortunately they seemed to all have places of their own to go.

We walked a block and a half before arriving at the girls' house, a place far better equipped for a private conversation than the guys'. There was no porch, open rooms, or privacy at the guys' house, it was just a big mess of a place with untrustworthy plumbing. The girls' house was not only known for exemplary plumbing, it also had a large courtyard in the back with a small office adjacent to it. The office was very private and well away from any potential interruptions. Scottie wanted to talk, I wanted to listen, and God was working in both of our lives.

The word basic doesn't even begin to describe the project office. An old desk, a couple of green leather-backed 1970's style chairs with little wheels, a few stacks of different colored paper, and a couple of random pens was about all you could find. There was, however, a small bookshelf filled with some really great books I am totally sure I undervalued.

We sat down in those old chairs across from each other, and Scottie leaned forward, elbows on his knees, with his head in hands. He didn't hold back his tears or frustrations while he walked me through what was happening and the deep sadness he felt for his family.

"I don't understand why life has to be so hard. Everything feels very broken," Scottie barely murmured, just as he finished sharing some of the details of what was troubling him.

"Man. I can't begin to tell you how sorry I am. I was having a bad night. I'd been a jerk, but now I'm so glad you found me out there. There is hope for me and you, Scottie. There's hope and love for your entire family, and God can do some pretty amazing things. He is the one who stands by me and helps me in times like this."

Scottie stared intently at me as I continued, "Through the life of Jesus, God offers us forgiveness, hope, and love. There's this thing called sin, though, and it stands in the way of all of this. The world says we can do what we want, but I think you know that's not how it works. God is awesome and perfect, and because of the problem of sin, we are completely separated from him. Jesus, however, changed everything. Because of Jesus, God created a path to him and he is willing to forgive us, if we mean it. I asked God earlier tonight to forgive me for screwing up at the dinner, and God promises in his word that he will forgive us. So, he forgave me! This world is a mess, right? We need hope, and because of Jesus, we have all of the hope and love this world could ever need."

"Hope. Hope seems pretty far away," Scottie said with more tears spilling down his cheeks.

"I know what you mean. I've been there, man."

"So, he will forgive me? You have no clue. It seems almost impossible God would want anything to do with me."

"Right, and I feel the same way! But the Bible tells us that with God, all things are possible, and this includes forgiving you and me. In a way, though, it makes complete sense. God loves you, man!"

We'd shared a lot, but the room suddenly got pretty silent for a few seconds. The chairs squeaked every so often as we started talking again in this old room in this old beach town. The empty walls and old furniture did just a good enough job to keep us focused and comfortable.

Lifting his head a little higher with a determined gleam in his eye, my friend Scottie said, "So, I want to do this. I want to ask God to forgive me and to follow Jesus. I'm done doing this all on my own."

As the minutes seemed to fly by, our wet eyes turned into slight smiles of delight and joy, and a new hope emerged in both of us as we joined hands, bowed our heads together, and prayed. Nothing else could be heard, just the soft voices of Scottie and me talking to our Father in Heaven, one of us embracing the truth about Jesus for the first time and the other grateful in praising our God who loves us so much. The mood in the office had moved from sadness to anticipation. God had brought two broken men together and bonded us both to him in different, yet the same ways.

Clouds covered the sky the next day and it looked like rain was on its way. Scottie and I met around 5:00 that evening in the same office. We joyfully experienced the scriptures together, affirming the decision Scottie had made, while laughing and sharing the excitement of the moment together. After about twenty minutes, I asked him if he would come out to the beach with me. I told Scottie we could go find another guy to share the love of God with, and he was surprisingly excited. I wasn't sure if he would be just a little nervous, but he told me he was ready to talk about Jesus with anyone who'd listen. We got up, exited the courtyard, and headed to the boardwalk.

We'd been strolling down the boardwalk for a few minutes when I noticed a young man in a shiny, green Seattle Supersonics jacket sitting alone on a bench not too far away. He was probably close to our age with a short haircut and a large duffle bag on the ground next to the bench. We approached him together, and I was thrilled that Scottie was going to be able to listen to me share the love of Jesus with this young man.

He looked up as we came close and I started us off by saying, 'Hey, how are…"

"I lived in Seattle for a few years!" Scottie exclaimed to the young man, completely cutting me off.

Scottie plopped right down on the bench next to him and began a conversation about Seattle with the young man, who introduced himself to us as Charles. Feeling a bit awkward and not sure what to say or do, I just quietly sat on the other side of the bench to listen and pray. They spent the next ten minutes talking about Seattle and traveling the country, and before I knew it, Scottie began to share almost verbatim what I had shared with him just last night. It felt weird to me that I wasn't doing the talking, and still not really knowing what to do, I began to silently pray in earnest for my friend who launched into the story of Jesus' life on this earth and what it all meant to him. He passionately shared with the green jacket guy about the love of God and how it might be hard to understand, but God had a plan and purpose for all of our lives. Charles listened intently and engaged in the discussion with Scottie, while I continued to sit there in dead silence, praying like crazy, and just taking in the wild scene.

Before I knew it, the three of us bowed our heads in prayer and Scottie led Charles into a relationship with Jesus. There were these crazy chills shooting up and down my spine. *Is this what it's like, God? Is this how we go and make disciples?* I could barely believe what had just happened, but I was very excited about the entire situation. God's grace was sufficient enough to allow me to be part of that moment with Scottie and Charles, and there was nowhere else in the world I would have rather been. To see both of their lives being changed, and to have God allow me to be close enough to see him work, was an absolutely brilliant blessing and one I will never forget. After Scottie finished praying, I wrapped our time up with a few thoughts and practical plans for Charles. I also had the chance to ask him more about his life.

"I'm just at the beginning of my journey," he said with a grin. "I'm traveling the US Seacoast for the next year or two." He went on to share his dreams of the journey, and we shared how God could impact it each day.

"God has changed all of us," I said enthusiastically. "He will be with you each step of the way, and, through the Bible, he will give you guidance and encouragement as you go, Charles."

Scottie had connected deeply with him, and it was a blast just to sit back as they shared their stories and laughed about their new lives.

"I don't suppose I'll see you two again," our friend, Charles, said.

"You never know, but probably not until we all die," said Scottie with a huge smile.

Charles, in his shiny green Supersonics jacket, got up and walked down the beach, disappearing only minutes after making a decision that would forever impact his life. Scottie and I stayed on that bench and watched the waves and talked for awhile. Eventually we meandered back to the project house. Once again in the simple office, we bowed our heads together in prayer for each other and for Charles.

"What's this?" Scottie asked me.

"This is your Bible, Scottie. I'm leaving tomorrow, and you'll need this," I told him as he stared at the large book.

He leaned over in his chair and gently pulled the book from my extended hands. Holding it lovingly, he stared at the cover like it was something he had never seen before. His fingers gently pushed opened the pages, and we walked through some of my favorite passages, especially focusing on some that would directly impact Scottie immediately. We talked about getting involved in a local church for support and encouragement, and I shared some important next steps in his new and exciting relationship with God. I hugged him, then he walked away and out of my life for the past twenty-five years.

The next morning, the sun rose gently behind me over the Atlantic, and one more time my packed-full, little, green Subaru GL Sport and I began the long trek home to Dayton, Ohio. The smell of salt air was soon exchanged for the odor of car fumes on the highway, and my warm views of the beach were traded for mountains. Those lush, green hills eventually gave way to the flatlands of the Midwest, and the same music that brought me to Virginia Beach took me safely home to Ohio.

That summer adventure of 1992 in Virginia Beach will always hold a place close to my heart, not only because I first met Melanie on those shores, but also because of what happened with Scottie. As high as my hopes may have been when I pulled out of my parents' driveway, I never dreamed my summer would end in such a dramatic fashion. God had stayed with me, even when I was a wreck and humiliated myself during my talk at the dinner, he was still with me. He knew what was going to happen, he allowed me to screw everything up, and he took my broken soul and brought me into something good and beautiful and eternal. To answer the call of the God of the Heavens, all I had to do was stand on a beach in my brokenness, and when the moment came, I had to be open to whatever might happen. I had to tell Scottie, "My time is yours".

It's funny, but God is always telling us, "My time is yours", isn't he? He is always here for us, capturing in his heart every word of prayer, every thought, and every deed you've ever done. He walks beside us when our friends fail us and we feel very alone. With God, we are never alone! Never! He stands by us when we are cornered in dark garages by bullies and can't find a way out. He's there when we race home to escape the kids chasing us, and instead of living in fear, he stokes our courage by giving us the real name he has for us - Lion Heart. He is there when our hearts are broken by the people we love the most, and when we feel alone and confused and there's just way more pain and tears than we've ever dreamed we'd see. God is right there with us when our friends think we've lost it and they go off to retire on beaches in Florida, while we choose to walk alone down the boardwalk and spend a decade of our lives telling strangers how much Jesus loves them. He is with us when we are so very broken and cry out the words of Jesus, "My God, my God, why have you forsaken me?" (Matthew 27:46). He's there to whisper into the deepest parts of our hearts, "The Lord will fight for you, and you have only to be silent" (Exodus 14:14). When we see no escape, and all of our failures collapse around us, God stands by with words of hope, breathing the most powerful courage into our hearts. When our world is spinning in chaos, and when it appears the devil may have finally won and broken us beyond what we thought could be broken, Jesus stands up and reminds us it isn't the first time the devil has broken someone. The devil thought he had doomed all of mankind for eternity, but he couldn't have been more wrong. Jesus! Jesus lived a broken yet glorious life, and it is in him we can put every ounce of our hope. Jesus experienced the greatest betrayal, the beatings from a powerful battalion, and the utter agony of death on a cross. The devil and almost everyone believed Jesus had been defeated, but all of this was part of God's plan for you, and for me. The life of Jesus was planned as God's greatest victory over suffering, over hopelessness, over sin, over the devil, and over death. God was with Jesus, and he is with you. He stands by you and is here for you now, no matter what you might be facing. He offers you hope, more love than you could ever imagine, and an eternity with him in paradise. He is your comforter, your counselor, and everything you could ever hope for in a God who loves and forgives you. You can boldly stand on this truth because of the life of Jesus and because of the presence of our loving God in your life. God loves you. God stands by you.

God is for you.

Acknowledgements

Have you seen the movie "Castaway"? So much of my story of writing this book was like living in the movie "Castaway". Too many times it seemed as if I'd been thrown auspiciously into isolation for an extended period of time, where the mind gets a little nutty, in a place where having a volleyball named Wilson as your best friend doesn't seem like too much of a stretch. For the past nineteen months you have might have caught me sitting alone inside Me & Ollies in Exeter, New Hampshire. Or you could have found me in our comfy red chair with my feet propped up on the ottoman in our living room, as a steaming coffee usually sat with reach. I spent a couple of days at the beach, but honestly the wind, the sand, the ocean, and the eclectic people around me were far too much of a distraction to engage my productivity. As the melancholy "Time" from the movie *Inception* played and replayed a thousand times into my headphones, here I've sat for more than a year and a half doing this thing. It seems very alone, until you open your eyes and suddenly you realize how many people actually brought you to this place, and into one of the greatest endings of something in your life. Those people are many, and I'll do my best to them due homage here.

None of this happens without the onslaught of support and encouragement of my best friend in this world, Melanie. You have the best heart of anyone I've ever met, and have inspired me and pushed me onward countless times over these nineteen months. Thank you to my editor, Carmen Palmquist, who has sacrificed far too much to help a virtually unknown writer do something he probably had no business doing. Thanks for believing in me and where this story was going. And thanks for forgiving me for all of those commas. If I was Frodo, she was Samwise. Also, a colossal thank you to my tenth grade English teacher, Mrs. Jennifer Pellish, who saw the potential in me before anyone else. It's teachers like you that truly make a difference, and I'm sure there are hundreds, maybe thousands of students who could say this about you. To J.R. Gwartney, you're the only one who could have written the foreward, and one of the best friends anyone could ever have. Thanks for taking this on despite never having written before (I told you that you would be a great writer one day!). Thank you to our children, who gave me the time and peace I needed to finish this story. Each of you are a blessing from God – Max, Kaitlin, Josh, Summer, Daniel, and Sammy. Thank you to my mom, for being the big hero in the worst moments of my life, and to my sister Michelle, who always believed the best in me, even when I didn't believe in myself.

And finally, to my friends who ignited this fire within me, and encouraged me for years to write this book share my story with the world, thank you. My most fitting words for you are the same used by Clarence the Angel from It's A Wonderful Life –

Dear George:—
Remember no man
is a failure who has
friends.

Thanks for the wings!
Love
Clarence

Made in the USA
Columbia, SC
29 December 2017